FAVORITE BRAND NAME™

SLOW COOKER

RECIPES

Publications International, Ltd.

Favorite Brand Name Recipes at www.fbnr.com

Favorite Brand Name is a trademark of Publications International, Ltd.

Recipe development:
Bev Bennett (pages 26, 88, 105, 158, 208, 210, 264, 272, 292, 296, 299, 302, 306, 344, 360).
Nicole Guagliardo (pages 12, 16, 18, 34, 54, 91, 96, 156, 161, 274, 276, 314, 316, 318, 328).
Nancy Hughes (pages 8, 12, 15, 86, 198, 204, 277, 290, 294, 300, 316, 364, 366, 367, 368).
Karen Levin (pages 20, 23, 30, 32, 36, 44, 94, 104, 154, 160, 268, 270, 298, 313, 324).
Margaret Maples (pages 58, 59, 115, 144, 173, 176, 202, 203, 214, 307, 312, 326, 328, 361, 366).
Marcia Stanley (pages 10, 14, 20, 30, 56, 73, 200, 218, 266, 274, 348, 349, 355, 364, 367).

Photography on pages 9, 10, 13, 16,19, 21, 26, 31, 35, 37, 55, 57, 87, 89, 95, 97, 155, 157, 159, 177, 199, 201, 205, 211, 219, 265, 267, 269, 271, 273, 275, 293, 295, 297, 303, 315, 317, 325, 345 and 365 by Proffitt Photography Ltd., Chicago.

Photographers: Laurie Proffitt, Cindy Trimm
Photographers' Assistant: Chad Evans
Prop Stylist: Paula Walters
Food Stylists: Carol Parik, Carol Smoler
Food Stylists' Assistant: Elaine Funk

Pictured on the front cover *(clockwise from top):* Saucy Tropical Turkey *(page 218),* Pork and Mushroom Ragout *(page 182) and* Italian-Style Pot Roast *(page 94).*

Pictured on the back cover *(clockwise from top):* Three Bean Mole Chili *(page 36),* Winter Squash and Apples *(page 314),* Mexicali Chicken *(page 198) and* Caribbean Sweet Potato & Bean Stew *(page 268).*

ISBN-13: 978-1-4127-2286-5
ISBN-10: 1-4127-2286-1

Library of Congress Control Number: 2005925713

Manufactured in China.

8 7 6 5 4 3 2 1

CONTENTS

Fiery Chile Beef, page 88

Creamy Artichoke-
Parmesan Dip, page 8

Shredded Apricot Pork
Sandwiches, page 294

Mexicali Chicken,
page 198

SLOW COOKING SECRETS

Slow Cooking 101

Slow cookers can prepare just about any type of food that you can imagine. Soups, stews, creative main dishes, party snacks, and yummy desserts are all included in this cookbook.

With the hectic pace of today's lifestyle, cooks have discovered this time-saving kitchen helper. Spend a few minutes preparing the ingredients, then turn on the slow cooker and relax. Low heat and long cooking times take the stress out of meal preparation. Leave for work or a day of leisure and come home 4, 8 or even 10 hours later to a hot, delicious meal.

The Benefits

- No need for constant attention or frequent stirring.
- No worry about burning.
- No sink full of pots and pans to scrub at the end of a long day.
- Provides an extra burner or oven for entertaining and holidays.
- Keeps your kitchen cool by keeping your oven turned off.
- Saves energy—cooking on LOW setting uses less energy than most light bulbs.

Simple Secrets

This book is chock-full of dozens of secrets to make slow cooking a success. For even greater success, keep in mind these few simple guidelines:

• Manufacturers recommend that slow cooker should be $^1/_2$ to $^3/_4$ full for best results.

• Keep the lid on!

• Because flavors often become diluted with long slow cooking, taste the finished dish before serving and adjust the seasonings to your preference.

• Slow cooking at high altitudes may take more time.

Meats and Poultry

• Use less tender, more inexpensive cuts of meat.

• Trim visible fat before putting meats in the slow cooker.

• Brown fatty cuts of meat, such as ribs and ground meats, to cook off excess fat before adding to the slow cooker.

• Brown meats and poultry before placing in the slow cooker to add more flavor and color.

• Use skinless cuts of poultry or remove skin before cooking and cut-up whole chicken before cooking it in the slow cooker.

Vegetables

• Root vegetables such as potatoes and carrots take longer to cooker than meat. Cut vegetables into small, uniform pieces and place near the bottom or the sides of the slow cooker.

• Thaw frozen vegetables before adding to the slow cooker. Frozen vegetables lengthen the cooking time and add extra moisture to the dish.

Reduce Fat and Thicken Juices

Because the slow cooker captures moisture, there may be excess cooking liquid at the end of the cooking time. Follow these easy steps to help reduce fat and thicken the juices.

• To easily remove most of the fat from the accumulated juices, remove the solids and let the liquid stand about 5 minutes so the fat can rise to the surface. Skim the fat with a large spoon.

• To thicken juices while the dish is cooking, add quick-cooking tapioca at the beginning of the cook time; the juice will thicken as the dish cooks.

• To thicken juices at the end of the cooking time, remove solid foods from the juices. Make a smooth paste of $^1/_4$ cup *each* flour and water or 2 tablespoons *each* cornstarch and water. Stir the paste into the cooking liquid. Turn the slow cooker to HIGH and cook about 15 minutes until the mixture boils and liquid thickens.

Food Safety Tips

• If you prepare ingredients in advance, be sure to cover and refrigerate the food until you are ready to start cooking. Store uncooked meats and vegetables separately.

• Do not reheat foods in the slow cooker.

• Do not use the slow cooker to defrost and cook frozen foods. Defrost them first in the refrigerator or microwave.

• Don't keep your finished dish in the slow cooker for long with the heat off.

Baking Basics

• At least one manufacturer sells special baking pans that fit inside its slow cooker. They are handy, but regular baking pans, casserole and soufflé dishes also work. Even coffee cans and soup cans work well in smaller 3-quart cookers. It is not necessary to place a trivet or some other "stand" under the bottom of the baking dish.

• Some recipes instruct the cook to leave the lid slightly ajar while cooking to prevent excess condensation from dripping on the food. Excess condensation can sometimes leave indentations on the top of baked goods that you may find undesirable.

Foil to the Rescue

To easily lift a dish or a meatloaf out of the slow cooker, make foil handles according to the following directions:

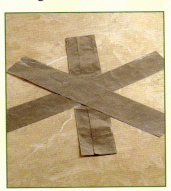

Photo 1: Tear off three 18×3-inch strips of heavy-duty foil. Crisscross strips so they resemble spokes of a wheel. Place your dish or food in the center of the strips.

Photo 2: Pull foil strips up and over and place into slow cooker. Leave them in while you cook so you can easily lift the item out again when it is ready.

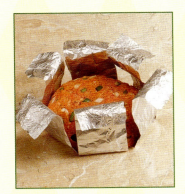

By following these simple techniques and using the exciting recipes in this cookbook, you will soon be preparing wonderful dishes with little effort.

No-Fuss
Snacks & Drinks

Creamy Artichoke-Parmesan Dip

    2 cans (14 ounces each) quartered artichokes, drained and chopped
    2 cups (8 ounces) shredded mozzarella cheese
  1½ cups grated Parmesan cheese
  1½ cups mayonnaise
   ½ cup finely chopped onion
   ½ teaspoon dried oregano leaves
   ¼ teaspoon garlic powder
    Pita wedges
    Assorted cut-up vegetables

1. Place all ingredients except pita wedges and vegetables into slow cooker; stir to blend well. Cover; cook on LOW 2 hours.

2. Serve with pita wedges and vegetables.

Makes 4 cups dip

Creamy Artichoke-Parmesan Dip

Pizza Fondue

½ pound bulk Italian sausage
1 cup chopped onion
2 jars (26 ounces each) pasta sauce
4 ounces thinly sliced ham, finely chopped
1 package (3 ounces) sliced pepperoni, finely chopped
¼ teaspoon red pepper flakes
1 pound mozzarella cheese, cut into ¾-inch cubes
1 loaf Italian or French bread, cut into 1-inch cubes

1. Cook sausage and onion in large skillet until sausage is browned. Drain off fat.

2. Transfer sausage mixture to slow cooker. Stir in pasta sauce, ham, pepperoni and pepper flakes. Cover; cook on LOW 3 to 4 hours.

3. Serve sauce with cheese cubes, bread cubes and fondue forks.

Makes 20 to 25 appetizer servings

Sausage Dip

1 pound bulk sausage, cooked
1 pound processed American cheese food, cut into 1-inch cubes
1 pound Mexican-flavored processed cheese food, cut into 1-inch cubes
1 can (16 ounces) refried beans
1 can (10¾ ounces) condensed cream of mushroom soup
1 small onion, chopped
Tortilla chips

Place all ingredients except tortilla chips into slow cooker. Cover; cook on LOW about 2 hours or until heated through. Serve with tortilla chips.

Makes 20 servings

Pizza Fondue

Parmesan Ranch Snack Mix

    3 cups bite-size corn or rice cereal
    2 cups oyster crackers
    1 package (5 ounces) bagel chips, broken in half
1½ cups pretzel twists
    1 cup shelled pistachios
    2 tablespoons grated Parmesan cheese
¼ cup butter, melted
    1 package (1 ounce) ranch salad dressing mix
½ teaspoon garlic powder

1. Combine cereal, oyster crackers, bagel chips, pretzels, pistachios and Parmesan cheese in slow cooker; mix gently.

2. Combine butter, salad dressing mix and garlic powder in small bowl. Pour over cereal mixture; toss lightly to coat. Cover; cook on LOW 3 hours. Remove cover and stir gently. Continue to cook, uncovered, on LOW 30 minutes. *Makes about 9½ cups snack mix*

Sweet and Spicy Sausage Rounds

    1 pound Kielbasa sausage, cut into ¼-inch rounds
⅔ cup blackberry jam
⅓ cup steak sauce
    1 tablespoon prepared mustard
½ teaspoon ground allspice

1. Place all ingredients in slow cooker; toss to coat completely. Cook on HIGH 3 hours or until richly glazed.

2. Serve with cocktail picks for appetizers or over rice tossed with chopped green onion for an entrée. *Makes 3 cups*

Parmesan Ranch Snack Mix

Cranberry-Barbecue Chicken Wings

      3 pounds chicken wings
        Salt and pepper
      1 container (12 ounces) cranberry-orange relish
      ½ cup barbecue sauce
      2 tablespoons quick-cooking tapioca
      1 tablespoon prepared mustard

1. Preheat broiler. Rinse chicken and pat dry. Cut off and discard wing tips. Cut each wing in half at joint. Place chicken on rack of broiler pan; season with salt and pepper. Broil 4 to 5 inches from heat for 10 to 12 minutes or until browned, turning once. Transfer chicken to slow cooker.

2. Stir together relish, barbecue sauce, tapioca and mustard in small bowl. Pour over chicken. Cover; cook on LOW 4 to 5 hours.   *Makes about 16 appetizer servings*

Bacon & Cheese Dip

      2 packages (8 ounces each) reduced-fat cream cheese, softened, cut into cubes
      4 cups shredded reduced-fat sharp Cheddar cheese
      1 cup fat-free evaporated milk
      2 tablespoons prepared mustard
      1 tablespoon chopped onion
      2 teaspoons Worcestershire sauce
      ½ teaspoon salt
      ¼ teaspoon hot pepper sauce
      1 pound turkey bacon, crisp-cooked and crumbled

Place cream cheese, Cheddar cheese, evaporated milk, mustard, onion, Worcestershire sauce, salt and pepper sauce into slow cooker. Cover; cook, stirring occasionally, on LOW 1 hour or until cheese melts. Stir in bacon; adjust seasonings. Serve with crusty bread or fruit and vegetable dippers.   *Makes about 4 cups*

Creamy Cheesy Spinach Dip

    2 packages (10 ounces each) frozen chopped spinach, thawed
    2 cups chopped onions
    1 teaspoon salt
    ½ teaspoon garlic powder
    ¼ teaspoon black pepper
   12 ounces processed cheese with jalapeño peppers, cubed
      Assorted crackers (optional)
      Cherry tomatoes with pulp removed (optional)

1. Drain spinach and squeeze dry, reserving ¾ cup liquid. Place spinach, reserved liquid, onions, salt, garlic powder and pepper into slow cooker; stir to blend. Cover; cook on HIGH 1½ hours.

2. Stir in cheese and cook 30 minutes longer or until melted. Serve with crackers or fill cherry tomato shells. *Makes about 4 cups dip*

Helpful Hint: To thaw spinach quickly, remove paper wrapper from spinach containers. Microwave at HIGH (100%) 3 to 4 minutes or until just thawed.

Reuben Dip

    1 jar or bag (25 to 28 ounces) sauerkraut, drained
    2 cups shredded Swiss cheese
    3 packages (2½ ounces each) corned beef, shredded
    ½ cup (1 stick) margarine, melted
    1 egg, beaten
      Rye cocktail bread or crackers

1. Combine all ingredients except rye bread in slow cooker. Cover; cook on HIGH 2 hours.

2. Serve with rye cocktail bread. *Makes 12 servings*

Honey-Mustard Chicken Wings

    3 pounds chicken wings
    1 teaspoon salt
    1 teaspoon black pepper
    ½ cup honey
    ½ cup barbecue sauce
    2 tablespoons spicy brown mustard
    1 clove garlic, minced
    3 to 4 thin lemon slices

1. Rinse chicken and pat dry. Cut off wing tips; discard. Cut each wing at joint to make two pieces. Sprinkle salt and pepper on both sides of chicken. Place wing pieces on broiler rack. Broil 4 to 5 inches from heat about 10 minutes, turning halfway through cooking. Place broiled chicken wings in slow cooker.

2. Combine honey, barbecue sauce, mustard and garlic in small bowl; mix well. Pour sauce over chicken wings. Top with lemon slices. Cover; cook on LOW 4 to 5 hours.

3. Remove and discard lemon slices. Serve wings with sauce. *Makes about 24 appetizers*

SLOW COOKING SECRET

Keep the lid on! The slow cooker can take as long as 30 minutes to regain heat lost when the cover is removed. Only remove the lid when instructed to do so by the recipes.

Honey-Mustard Chicken Wings

Easy Taco Dip

½ **pound ground chuck**
1 **cup frozen corn**
½ **cup chopped onion**
½ **cup salsa**
½ **cup mild taco sauce**
1 **can (4 ounces) diced mild green chilies**
1 **can (4 ounces) sliced ripe olives, drained**
1 **cup (4 ounces) shredded Mexican blend cheese**
Tortilla chips
Sour cream

1. Cook meat in large nonstick skillet over medium-high until no longer pink, stirring to separate; drain. Spoon into slow cooker.

2. Add corn, onion, salsa, taco sauce, chilies and olives to slow cooker; stir to combine. Cover; cook on LOW 2 to 4 hours.

3. Just before serving, stir in cheese. Serve with tortilla chips and sour cream.

Makes about 3 cups dip

Serving Suggestion: To keep this dip hot through your entire party, simply leave it in the slow cooker on LOW.

Easy Taco Dip

Maple-Glazed Meatballs

1½ cups ketchup
1 cup maple syrup or maple-flavored syrup
⅓ cup reduced-sodium soy sauce
1 tablespoon quick-cooking tapioca
1½ teaspoons ground allspice
1 teaspoon dry mustard
2 packages (about 16 ounces each) frozen fully-cooked meatballs
1 can (20 ounces) pineapple chunks, drained

1. Stir together ketchup, syrup, soy sauce, tapioca, allspice and mustard in slow cooker.

2. Separate meatballs. Carefully stir meatballs and pineapple chunks into ketchup mixture. Cover; cook on LOW 5 to 6 hours. Stir before serving. Serve with cocktail picks.

Makes about 48 meatballs

Variation: Serve over hot cooked rice for an entrée.

Spicy Sweet & Sour Cocktail Franks

2 packages (8 ounces each) cocktail franks
½ cup ketchup or chili sauce
½ cup apricot preserves
1 teaspoon hot pepper sauce
Additional hot pepper sauce, if desired

1. Combine all ingredients in slow cooker; mix well. Cover; cook on LOW 2 to 3 hours.

2. Serve warm or at room temperature with cocktail picks and additional hot pepper sauce, if desired.

Makes about 4 dozen cocktail franks

Maple-Glazed Meatballs

Honey-Sauced Chicken Wings

3 pounds chicken wings
1 teaspoon salt
½ teaspoon black pepper
1 cup honey
½ cup soy sauce
¼ cup ketchup
¼ cup chopped onions
2 tablespoons oil
2 cloves garlic, minced
¼ teaspoon red pepper flakes
Toasted sesame seeds (optional)

1. Rinse chicken and pat dry. Cut off and discard wing tips. Cut each wing at joint to make two sections. Sprinkle wing parts with salt and pepper. Place wings on broiler pan. Broil 4 to 5 inches from heat 20 minutes, 10 minutes a side or until chicken is brown. Place chicken into slow cooker.

2. For sauce, combine honey, soy sauce, ketchup, onions, oil, garlic and pepper flakes in bowl. Pour over chicken wings. Cover; cook on LOW 4 to 5 hours or on HIGH 2 to 2½ hours. Garnish with sesame seeds, if desired.

Makes about 32 appetizers

Chunky Pinto Bean Dip

2 cans (15 ounces each) pinto beans, rinsed and drained
1 can (14½ ounces) salsa-style diced tomatoes, drained
1 cup chopped onion
⅔ cup chunky salsa
1 tablespoon vegetable oil
1½ teaspoons minced garlic
1 teaspoon ground coriander
1 teaspoon ground cumin
1½ cups (6 ounces) shredded Mexican cheese blend or Cheddar cheese
¼ cup chopped cilantro
   Blue corn tortilla chips or tortilla chips
   Assorted raw vegetables

1. Combine beans, tomatoes, onion, salsa, oil, garlic, coriander and cumin in slow cooker. Cover; cook on LOW 5 to 6 hours or until onion is tender.

2. Partially mash bean mixture with potato masher. Stir in cheese and cilantro. Serve at room temperature with chips and vegetables. *Makes about 5 cups dip*

SLOW COOKING SECRET

For a party, use a small-sized slow cooker (1 quart) on the low setting to keep hot dips warm.

Hearty Calico Bean Dip

 ¾ pound ground beef, cooked and drained
 ½ pound sliced bacon, crisp-cooked and crumbled
 1 can (16 ounces) baked beans
 1 can (15½ ounces) Great Northern beans, rinsed and drained
 1 can (15 ounces) kidney beans, rinsed and drained
 1 small onion, chopped
 ½ cup brown sugar
 ½ cup ketchup
 1 tablespoon vinegar
 1 teaspoon prepared mustard
   Tortilla chips

Combine all ingredients except tortilla chips in large bowl; place into slow cooker. Cover; cook on LOW 4 hours or on HIGH 2 hours. Serve with tortilla chips. *Makes 12 servings*

Curried Snack Mix

 3 tablespoons butter
 2 tablespoons packed light brown sugar
 1½ teaspoons hot curry powder
 ¼ teaspoon salt
 ¼ teaspoon ground cumin
 2 cups rice squares cereal
 1 cup walnut halves
 1 cup dried cranberries

Melt butter in large skillet. Add brown sugar, curry powder, salt and cumin; mix well. Add cereal, walnuts and cranberries; stir to coat. Spoon mixture into slow cooker. Cover; cook on LOW 3 hours. Remove cover; cook an additional 30 minutes. *Makes 16 servings*

Hearty Calico Bean Dip

Mulled Cranberry Tea

2 tea bags
1 cup boiling water
1 bottle (48 ounces) cranberry juice
½ cup dried cranberries
⅓ cup sugar
1 large lemon, cut into ¼-inch slices
4 cinnamon sticks
6 whole cloves
   Additional thin lemon slices
   Additional cinnamon sticks

1. Place tea bags in slow cooker. Pour boiling water over tea bags; cover and let stand 5 minutes. Remove and discard tea bags. Stir in cranberry juice, cranberries, sugar, lemon slices, 4 cinnamon sticks and cloves. Cover; cook on HIGH 1 to 2 hours or on LOW 2 to 3 hours.

2. Remove and discard lemon slices, cinnamon sticks and cloves. Serve in warm mug with additional fresh lemon slice and cinnamon stick.

Makes 8 servings

Mulled Cranberry Tea

Triple Delicious Hot Chocolate

⅓ **cup sugar**
¼ **cup unsweetened cocoa powder**
¼ **teaspoon salt**
 3 **cups milk, divided**
¾ **teaspoon vanilla**
 1 **cup heavy cream**
 1 **square (1 ounce) bittersweet chocolate**
 1 **square (1 ounce) white chocolate**
¾ **cup whipped cream**
 6 **teaspoons mini chocolate chips or shaved bittersweet chocolate**

1. Combine sugar, cocoa, salt and ½ cup milk in medium bowl. Beat until smooth. Pour into slow cooker. Add remaining 2½ cups milk and vanilla. Cover; cook on LOW 2 hours.

2. Add cream. Cover and cook on LOW 10 minutes. Stir in bittersweet and white chocolates until melted.

3. Pour hot chocolate into 6 coffee cups. Top each with 2 tablespoons whipped cream and 1 teaspoon chocolate chips.

Makes 6 servings

Triple Delicious Hot Chocolate

Chai Tea

    2 quarts (8 cups) water
    8 bags black tea
    ¾ cup granulated sugar*
    16 whole cloves
    16 whole cardamom seeds, pods removed (optional)
    5 cinnamon sticks
    8 slices fresh ginger
    1 cup milk

Chai Tea is typically a sweet drink. For less sweet tea, reduce sugar to ½ cup.

1. Combine all ingredients except milk in slow cooker. Cover; cook on HIGH 2 to 2½ hours.

2. Strain mixture; discard solids. (At this point, tea may covered and refrigerated up to 3 days).

3. Stir in milk just before serving. Serve warm or chilled.   *Makes 8 to 10 servings*

Spiced Citrus Tea

    4 tea bags
    Peel of 1 orange
    4 cups boiling water
    3 tablespoons honey
    2 cans (6 ounces each) orange-pineapple juice
    3 star anise
    3 cinnamon sticks
    Strawberries, raspberries or kiwis (optional)

1. Place tea bags and orange peel in slow cooker. Pour in boiling water. Cover and let steep 10 minutes. Discard tea bags and orange peel.

2. Add remaining ingredients to slow cooker. Cover; cook on LOW 3 hours. Garnish with strawberries, raspberries or kiwis, if desired.   *Makes 6 servings*

Warm & Spicy Fruit Punch

     4 cinnamon sticks
     1 orange
     1 teaspoon whole allspice
     ½ teaspoon whole cloves
     7 cups water
     1 can (12 ounces) frozen cranberry-raspberry juice concentrate, thawed
     1 can (6 ounces) frozen lemonade concentrate, thawed
     2 cans (5½ ounces each) apricot nectar

1. Break cinnamon into pieces. Using vegetable peeler, remove strips of orange peel. Squeeze juice from orange. Set aside.

2. Tie cinnamon, orange peel, allspice, and cloves in a cheesecloth bag.

3. Combine reserved orange juice, water, concentrates and apricot nectar in slow cooker; add spice bag. Cover; cook on LOW 5 to 6 hours.

4. Remove and discard spice bag.   *Makes about 14 (6-ounce) servings*

SLOW COOKING SECRET

Consider using your slow cooker as an "extra" burner when entertaining. For example, the slow cooker keeps beverages warm while other dishes are being prepared on top of the range.

SIMMERING SOUPS

Simmering Hot & Sour Soup

2 cans (14½ ounces each) chicken broth
1 cup chopped cooked chicken or pork
4 ounces fresh shiitake mushroom caps, thinly sliced
½ cup sliced bamboo shoots, cut into thin strips
3 tablespoons rice or rice wine vinegar
2 tablespoons soy sauce
1½ teaspoons chili paste *or* 1 teaspoon hot chili oil
4 ounces firm tofu, well drained and cut into ½-inch pieces
2 teaspoons Asian sesame oil
2 tablespoons cornstarch
2 tablespoons cold water
Chopped cilantro or sliced green onions

1. Combine chicken broth, chicken, mushrooms, bamboo shoots, vinegar, soy sauce and chili paste in slow cooker. Cover; cook on LOW for 3 to 4 hours.

2. Stir in tofu and sesame oil. Combine cornstarch with water; mix well. Stir into soup. Cover; cook on HIGH 10 minutes or until soup is thickened.

3. Serve hot; garnish with cilantro.

Makes 4 servings

Simmering Hot & Sour Soup

Chicken and Wild Rice Soup

   3 cans (14½ ounces each) chicken broth
   1 pound boneless skinless chicken breasts or thighs, cut into bite-size pieces
   1 package (6 ounces) converted long grain and wild rice mix with seasoning
      packet (not quick-cooking or instant rice)
   2 cups water
   1 cup sliced celery
   1 cup diced carrots
  ½ cup chopped onion
   1 tablespoon dried parsley flakes
  ½ teaspoon black pepper

Combine all ingredients in slow cooker; mix well. Cover; cook on LOW 6 to 7 hours or on HIGH 4 to 5 hours. *Makes 9 (1½ cups) servings*

Simple Hamburger Soup

   2 pounds ground beef or turkey, cooked and drained
   1 can (28 ounces) whole tomatoes, undrained
   2 cans (14 ounces each) beef broth
   1 bag (10 ounces) frozen gumbo soup vegetables
  ½ cup uncooked barley
   1 teaspoon salt
   1 teaspoon dried thyme leaves
    Black pepper

Combine all ingredients in slow cooker. Add water to cover. Cover; cook on HIGH 3 to 4 hours or until barley and vegetables are tender. *Makes 8 servings*

Variations: Add other frozen or canned vegetables or extra diced potatoes and carrots. Diced or stewed tomatoes can be substituted for the whole tomatoes.

Chicken and Wild Rice Soup

Three Bean Mole Chili

1 can (15 ounces) pinto beans, rinsed and drained
1 can (15 ounces) chili beans in spicy sauce, undrained
1 can (15 ounces) black beans, rinsed and drained
1 can (14½ ounces) Mexican or chili-style diced tomatoes, undrained
1 large green bell pepper, diced
1 small onion, diced
½ cup beef, chicken or vegetable broth
¼ cup prepared mole paste*
2 teaspoons ground cumin
2 teaspoons ground coriander (optional)
2 teaspoons chili powder
2 teaspoons minced garlic
   Toppings: Crushed tortilla chips, chopped cilantro or shredded cheese (optional)

*Mole paste is available in the Mexican section of large supermarkets or in specialty markets.

1. Combine all ingredients except toppings in slow cooker; mix well. Cover; cook on LOW 5 to 6 hours or until vegetables are tender.

2. Serve with toppings, if desired. *Makes 4 to 6 servings*

Three Bean Mole Chili

Clam Chowder

    5 cans (10¾ ounces each) condensed low-fat cream of potato soup
    2 cans (12 ounces each) evaporated skim milk
    2 cans (10 ounces each) whole clams, rinsed and drained
    1 can (14¾ ounces) cream-style corn
    2 cans (4 ounces each) tiny shrimp, rinsed and drained
    ¾ cup crisp-cooked and crumbled bacon (about ½ pound) or imitation
        bacon bits
    Lemon pepper to taste
    Oyster crackers

Combine all ingredients except crackers in slow cooker. Cover; cook on LOW 3 to 4 hours, stirring occasionally. Serve with oyster crackers.   *Makes 10 servings*

Quickie Vegetable-Beef Soup

    1 tablespoon vegetable oil
    1 to 2 pounds cubed beef or beef for stew
    3 cans (15 ounces each) mixed vegetables
    2 cans (10¾ ounces) golden mushroom soup
    1 can (14½ ounces) stewed tomatoes, undrained
    1 beef bouillon cube
    1 tablespoon Worcestershire sauce
    1 medium onion, chopped
     Salt
     Black pepper
    1 bay leaf

1. Heat oil in large skillet over medium-low heat; brown beef on all sides. Drain excess fat.

2. Combine all ingredients in slow cooker; mix thoroughly. Cover; cook on LOW 6 to 8 hours. Removed and discard bay leaf.   *Makes 10 servings*

Clam Chowder

Roast Tomato-Basil Soup

    2 cans (28 ounces each) peeled whole tomatoes, drained, seeded and
      liquid reserved
2½ tablespoons packed dark brown sugar
    1 medium onion, finely chopped
    3 cups tomato liquid reserved from canned tomatoes
    3 cups chicken broth
    3 tablespoons tomato paste
    ¼ teaspoon ground allspice
    1 can (5 ounces) evaporated milk
    ¼ cup shredded fresh basil leaves (about 10 large)
      Salt and black pepper

1. To roast tomatoes, preheat oven to 450°F. Line cookie sheet with foil; spray with nonstick cooking spray. Arrange tomatoes on foil in single layer. Sprinkle with brown sugar and top with onion. Bake about 25 to 30 minutes or until tomatoes look dry and light brown. Let tomatoes cool slightly; finely chop.

2. Place tomato mixture, 3 cups reserved liquid, chicken broth, tomato paste and allspice into slow cooker. Mix well. Cover; cook on LOW 8 hours or on HIGH 4 hours.

3. Add evaporated milk and basil; season with salt and pepper. Cook 30 minutes or until hot. Garnish as desired.

Makes 6 servings

Roast Tomato-Basil Soup

Hearty Chili Mac

- 1 pound lean ground beef
- 1 can (14½ ounces) diced tomatoes, drained
- 1 cup chopped onion
- 1 tablespoon chili powder
- 1 clove garlic, minced
- ½ teaspoon salt
- ½ teaspoon ground cumin
- ½ teaspoon dried oregano leaves
- ¼ teaspoon red pepper flakes
- ¼ teaspoon black pepper
- 2 cups cooked macaroni

Crumble ground beef into slow cooker. Add remaining ingredients except macaroni to slow cooker. Cover; cook on LOW 4 hours. Stir in cooked macaroni. Cover; cook on LOW 1 hour.

Makes 4 servings

SLOW COOKING SECRET

Cooking times are guidelines. Slow cookers, just like ovens, cook differently depending on heating units. You may need to slightly adjust the cooking times for your slow cooker.

Hearty Chili Mac

Pasta Fagioli Soup

2 cans (14½ ounces each) reduced-sodium beef broth
1 can (16 ounces) Great Northern beans, rinsed and drained
1 can (14½ ounces) diced tomatoes, undrained
2 medium zucchini, quartered lengthwise and sliced
1 tablespoon olive oil
1½ teaspoons minced garlic
½ teaspoon dried basil leaves
½ teaspoon dried oregano leaves
½ cup tubetti, ditilini or small shell pasta, uncooked
½ cup garlic seasoned croutons
½ cup grated Asiago or Romano cheese
3 tablespoons chopped fresh basil or Italian parsley (optional)

1. Combine broth, beans, tomatoes with juice, zucchini, oil, garlic, dried basil and oregano in slow cooker; mix well. Cover; cook on LOW 3 to 4 hours.

2. Stir in pasta. Cover; continue cooking on LOW 1 hour or until pasta is tender.

3. Serve soup with croutons and cheese. Garnish with fresh basil, if desired.

Makes 5 to 6 servings

Hearty Mushroom and Barley Soup

9 cups chicken broth
1 pound fresh mushrooms, sliced
1 large onion, chopped
2 carrots, peeled and chopped
2 ribs celery, chopped
½ cup pearled barley
½ ounce dried porcini mushrooms
3 cloves garlic, minced
1 teaspoon salt
½ teaspoon dried thyme leaves
½ teaspoon black pepper

Combine all ingredients in slow cooker. Cover; cook on LOW 4 to 6 hours.

Makes 8 to 10 servings

Variation: Add a beef or ham bone to slow cooker with the rest of the ingredients.

SLOW COOKING SECRET

Because herbs and spices tend to lose flavor in the slow cooker, you may prefer to adjust seasonings or add herbs and spices just before serving.

Easy Vegetarian Vegetable Bean Soup

    3 cans (14 ounces each) vegetable broth
    2 cups cubed unpeeled potatoes
    2 cups sliced leeks, white part only (about 3 medium)
    1 can (14½ ounces) diced tomatoes, undrained
    1 medium onion, chopped
    1 cup chopped or shredded cabbage
    1 cup sliced celery
    1 cup sliced peeled carrots
    3 cloves garlic, chopped
    ⅛ teaspoon dried rosemary
    1 can (16 ounces) white beans, drained
    Salt and black pepper

1. Combine all ingredients except beans, salt and pepper in slow cooker. Cover; cook on LOW 8 hours.

2. Stir in beans and season with salt and pepper. Cover; cook about 30 minutes or until beans are heated through.

Makes 10 servings

Easy Vegetarian Vegetable Bean Soup

Rustic Vegetable Soup

    1 jar (16 ounces) picante sauce
    1 package (10 ounces) frozen mixed vegetables, thawed
    1 package (10 ounces) frozen cut green beans, thawed
    1 can (10 ounces) condensed beef broth, undiluted
    1 to 2 baking potatoes, cut in ½-inch pieces
    1 medium green bell pepper, chopped
    ½ teaspoon sugar
    ¼ cup finely chopped fresh parsley

Combine all ingredients except parsley in slow cooker. Cover; cook on LOW 8 hours or on HIGH 4 hours. Stir in parsley; serve. *Makes 8 servings*

Easy Chili

    1 teaspoon vegetable oil
    1 pound extra-lean ground beef
    1 medium onion, chopped
    2 cans (10¾ ounces each) condensed tomato soup
    1 cup water
      Salt
      Black pepper
      Chili powder

1. Heat oil in large skillet over medium-high heat. Brown beef and onion. Drain excess fat.

2. Place meat mixture, soup, water, salt, pepper and chili powder to taste into slow cooker. Cover; cook on LOW 6 hours. *Makes 4 servings*

Serving Suggestion: Garnish with shredded cheese and serve with crackers or thick slices of Italian bread.

Rustic Vegetable Soup

Hamburger Soup

    1 pound lean ground beef
    1 envelope (1 ounce) dried onion soup mix
    1 envelope (1 ounce) Italian seasoning mix
    ¼ teaspoon seasoned salt
    ¼ teaspoon black pepper
    3 cups boiling water
    1 can (8 ounces) diced tomatoes, undrained
    1 can (8 ounces) tomato sauce
    1 tablespoon soy sauce
    1 cup sliced celery
    1 cup thinly sliced carrots
    2 cups cooked macaroni
    ¼ cup grated Parmesan cheese
    2 tablespoons chopped fresh parsley

1. Brown beef in medium skillet over medium-high heat; drain. Add beef, soup mix, Italian seasoning mix, seasoned salt and pepper to slow cooker. Stir in water, tomatoes with juice, tomato sauce and soy sauce. Add celery and carrots. Cover; cook on LOW 6 to 8 hours.

2. Increase heat to HIGH; stir in cooked macaroni and Parmesan cheese. Cover; cook 10 to 15 minutes. Sprinkle with parsley just before serving.   *Makes 6 to 8 servings*

Hamburger Soup

Easy Italian Vegetable Soup

 1 can (14½ ounces) diced tomatoes, undrained
 1 can (10½ ounces) condensed beef broth, undiluted
 1 package (8 ounces) sliced mushrooms
 1 medium yellow onion, chopped
 1 medium zucchini, thinly sliced
 1 medium green bell pepper, chopped
 ⅓ cup dry red wine or beef broth
 1½ tablespoons dried basil leaves
 2½ teaspoons sugar
 1 tablespoon extra virgin olive oil
 ½ teaspoon salt
 1 cup (4 ounces) shredded Mozzarella cheese (optional)

1. Combine tomatoes with juice, broth, mushrooms, onion, zucchini, bell pepper, wine, basil and sugar in slow cooker. Cover; cook on LOW 8 hours or on HIGH 4 hours.

2. Stir oil and salt into soup. Serve; garnish with cheese, if desired.   *Makes 5 to 6 servings*

Easy Italian Vegetable Soup

Peppery Potato Soup

2 cans (14½ ounces each) chicken broth
4 small baking potatoes, halved and sliced
1 large onion, quartered and sliced
1 rib celery with leaves, sliced
¼ cup all-purpose flour
¾ teaspoon black pepper
½ teaspoon salt
1 cup half and half
1 tablespoon butter
  Celery leaves or fresh parsley

1. Combine broth, potatoes, onion, celery, flour, pepper and salt in slow cooker; mix well. Cover; cook on LOW 6 to 7½ hours.

2. Stir in half and half; cover and continue to cook 1 hour.

3. Remove slow cooker lid. Slightly crush potato mixture with potato masher. Continue to cook, uncovered, an additional 30 minutes until slightly thickened. Just before serving, stir in butter. Garnish with celery leaves; if desired.   *Makes 6 (1¼ cup) servings*

Peppery Potato Soup

Italian Beef and Barley Soup

  1½ pounds boneless beef sirloin steak
    1 tablespoon vegetable oil
    4 medium carrots or parsnips, sliced ¼-inch thick
    1 cup chopped onion
    1 teaspoon dried thyme leaves
   ½ teaspoon dried rosemary
   ¼ teaspoon black pepper
   ⅓ cup pearl barley
    2 cans (14½ ounces each) beef broth
    1 can (14½ ounces) diced tomatoes with Italian seasoning, undrained

1. Cut meat into 1-inch pieces. Heat oil over medium-high heat in large skillet and brown beef on all sides. Set aside.

2. Place carrots and onion into slow cooker; sprinkle with thyme, rosemary and pepper. Top with barley and meat. Pour broth and tomatoes with juice over meat. Cover; cook on LOW 8 to 10 hours.

Makes 6 servings

Italian Beef and Barley Soup

Simmered Split Pea Soup

      3 cans (14½ ounces each) chicken broth
      1 package (16 ounces) dry split peas
      1 medium onion, diced
      2 medium carrots, diced
      1 teaspoon black pepper
      ½ teaspoon dried thyme leaves
      1 bay leaf
      8 slices bacon, crisp-cooked and crumbled, divided

1. Place broth, split peas, onion, carrots, pepper, thyme, bay leaf and half of crumbled bacon in slow cooker. Cover; cook on LOW 6 to 8 hours.

2. Remove bay leaf and adjust seasonings, if desired. Garnish with remaining bacon.

Makes 6 servings

Vegetable Beef Soup

      3 pounds beef for stew
      3 medium potatoes, diced
      3 medium onions, diced
      4 ribs celery, sliced
      4 carrots, sliced
      4 beef bouillon cubes
      2 teaspoons salt
      1 teaspoon black pepper
      5 cups water
      1 can (28 ounces) vegetable juice cocktail
      2 packages (10 ounces each) frozen mixed vegetables, thawed

1. Place all ingredients in order listed above except frozen vegetables in slow cooker. Cover; cook on LOW 8 to 10 hours or on HIGH 4 to 6 hours.

2. Add vegetables during last 2 hours of cooking.

Makes 8 servings

Easy Corn Chowder

2 cans (14½ ounces each) chicken broth
1 bag (16 ounces) frozen corn kernels
3 small potatoes, peeled and cut into ½-inch pieces
1 red bell pepper, diced
1 medium onion, diced
1 rib celery, sliced
½ teaspoon salt
½ teaspoon black pepper
¼ teaspoon ground coriander
½ cup heavy cream
8 slices bacon, crisp-cooked and crumbled

1. Place broth, corn, potatoes, bell pepper, onion, celery, salt, black pepper and coriander into slow cooker. Cover; cook on LOW 7 to 8 hours.

2. Partially mash soup mixture with potato masher to thicken. Stir in cream; cook on HIGH, uncovered, until hot. Adjust seasonings, if desired. Garnish with bacon.   *Makes 6 servings*

SLOW COOKING SECRET

Cut ingredients into uniform pieces so that everything cooks evenly.

Slow Cooker Cheese Soup

    2 cans (10¾ ounces each) condensed cream of celery soup
    4 cups(1 pound) shredded Cheddar cheese
    1 teaspoon paprika
    1 teaspoon Worcestershire sauce
1¼ cups half-and-half
    Salt and black pepper

Combine soup, cheese, paprika and Worcestershire sauce in slow cooker. Cover; cook on LOW 2 to 3 hours. Add half-and-half; stir to combine. Cover; cook another 20 minutes. Season with salt and pepper to taste. Garnish as desired. *Makes 4 servings*

Bobbie's Vegetable Hamburger Soup

    1 teaspoon vegetable oil
    1 pound extra-lean ground beef
    2 cans (14½ ounces each) seasoned diced tomatoes, undrained
    1 package (16 ounces) frozen vegetable blend
    2 cups water
    1 can (10¾ ounces) condensed tomato soup
    1 envelope (1 ounce) dried onion soup mix
    1 teaspoon sugar

1. Heat oil in large skillet over medium-low heat. Cook beef until no longer pink. Drain excess fat.

2. Place cooked ground beef and remaining ingredients into slow cooker; stir together. Cover; cook on LOW 6 to 8 hours. *Makes 4 servings*

Variation: Substitute ground turkey for ground beef.

Slow Cooker Cheese Soup

Potato-Crab Chowder

1 package (10 ounces) frozen corn
1 cup frozen hash brown potatoes
¾ cup finely chopped carrots
1 teaspoon dried thyme leaves
¾ teaspoon garlic-pepper seasoning
3 cups fat-free reduced-sodium chicken broth
½ cup water
1 cup evaporated milk
3 tablespoons cornstarch
1 can (6 ounces) crabmeat, drained
½ cup sliced green onions

1. Place corn, potatoes and carrots in slow cooker. Sprinkle with thyme and garlic-pepper seasoning. Add broth and water. Cover; cook on LOW 3½ to 4½ hours.

2. Stir together evaporated milk and cornstarch in medium bowl. Stir into slow cooker. Cover; cook on HIGH 1 hour. Just before serving, stir in crabmeat and green onions. Garnish as desired.

Makes 5 servings

Potato-Crab Chowder

Creamy Turkey Soup

2 cans (10½ ounces each) condensed cream of chicken soup
2 cups chopped cooked turkey breast meat
1 package (8 ounces) sliced mushrooms
1 medium yellow onion, chopped
1 teaspoon rubbed sage *or* ½ teaspoon dried poultry seasoning
1 cup frozen peas, thawed
½ cup milk
1 jar (about 4 ounces) diced pimiento

1. Combine soup, turkey, mushrooms, onion and sage in slow cooker. Cover; cook on LOW 8 hours or on HIGH 4 hours.

2. If cooking on LOW, turn to HIGH; stir in peas, milk and pimientos. Cook an additional 10 minutes or until heated through. *Makes 5 to 6 servings*

White Bean and Green Chili Pepper Soup

2 cans (15 ounces each) Great Northern beans, rinsed and drained
1 can (14½ ounces) fat-free chicken broth
1 cup finely chopped yellow onion
1 can (4½ ounces) diced green chilies
1 teaspoon ground cumin, divided
½ teaspoon garlic powder
¼ cup chopped fresh cilantro leaves
1 tablespoon extra virgin olive oil
⅓ cup sour cream (optional)

1. Combine beans, chicken broth, onion, chilies, ½ teaspoon cumin and garlic powder in slow cooker. Cover; cook on LOW 8 hours or on HIGH 4 hours.

2. Stir in cilantro, olive oil and remaining ½ teaspoon cumin. Garnish with sour cream, if desired. *Makes 5 servings*

Creamy Turkey Soup

Sausage, Butter Bean and Cabbage Soup

2 tablespoons butter, divided
1 large onion, chopped
12 ounces smoked sausage such as kielbasa or andouille, cut into ½-inch slices
8 cups chicken broth
½ head Savoy cabbage, shredded
3 tablespoons tomato paste
1 bay leaf
4 medium tomatoes, chopped
2 cans (14 ounces each) butter beans, drained
Salt and black pepper

1. Melt 1 tablespoon butter in large skillet over medium heat. Add onion; cook and stir 3 to 4 minutes or until golden. Place into slow cooker.

2. Melt remaining 1 tablespoon butter in the same skillet; cook sausage until brown on both sides. Add to slow cooker.

3. Place chicken broth, cabbage, tomato paste and bay leaf in slow cooker; stir well to combine. Cover; cook on LOW 4 hours or HIGH 2 hours.

4. Add tomatoes and beans; season with salt and pepper. Cover; cook 1 hour until heated through. Remove and discard bay leaf. *Makes 6 servings*

Note: Savoy cabbage is an excellent cooking cabbage with a full head of crinkled leaves varying from dark to pale green. Green cabbage may be substituted.

Sausage, Butter Bean and Cabbage Soup

1-2-3-4 Chili

2 pounds ground beef, browned and drained of fat
3 cans (15 ounces each) chili-spiced kidney beans, undrained
4 cans (8 ounces each) tomato sauce
Shredded Cheddar cheese (optional)
Green onions, sliced (optional)

Combine all ingredients in slow cooker. Cover; cook on LOW 6 to 8 hours. Garnish with cheese and sliced green onion, if desired.

Makes 8 servings

Serving Suggestion: Serve with cornbread.

Double Thick Baked Potato-Cheese Soup

2 pounds baking potatoes, peeled and cut into ½-inch cubes
2 cans (10½ ounces each) condensed cream of mushroom soup
1½ cups finely chopped green onions, divided
¼ teaspoon garlic powder
⅛ teaspoon ground red pepper
1½ cups (6 ounces) shredded sharp Cheddar cheese
1 cup (8 ounces) sour cream
1 cup milk
Black pepper

1. Combine potatoes, soup, 1 cup green onions, garlic powder and red pepper in slow cooker. Cover; cook on HIGH 4 hours or on LOW 8 hours.

2. Add cheese, sour cream and milk; stir until cheese has completely melted. Cover; cook on HIGH an additional 10 minutes. Season to taste with black pepper. Garnish with remaining green onions.

Makes 7 servings

1-2-3-4 Chili

Farmhouse Ham and Vegetable Chowder

2 cans (10½ ounces each) condensed cream of celery soup
2 cups diced cooked ham
1 package (10 ounces) frozen corn
1 large baking potato, cut in ½-inch pieces
1 medium red bell pepper, diced
½ teaspoon dried thyme leaves
2 cups small broccoli florets
½ cup milk

1. Combine all ingredients except broccoli and milk in slow cooker; stir to blend. Cover; cook on LOW 6 to 8 hours or on HIGH 3 to 4 hours.

2. If cooking on LOW, turn to HIGH; stir in broccoli and milk. Cover; cook 15 minutes or until broccoli is crisp tender. *Makes 6 servings*

Farmhouse Ham and Vegetable Chowder

Tuscan White Bean Soup

    6 ounces bacon, diced
10 cups chicken broth
   1 bag (1 pound) dried Great Northern beans, rinsed
   1 can (14½ ounces) diced tomatoes, undrained
   1 large onion, chopped
   3 carrots, peeled and chopped
   4 cloves garlic, minced
   1 fresh rosemary sprig *or* 1 teaspoon dried rosemary
   1 teaspoon black pepper

Cook bacon in medium skillet over medium-high heat until just cooked; drain and transfer to slow cooker. Add remaining ingredients. Cover; cook on LOW 8 hours or until beans are tender. Remove and discard rosemary sprig before serving.   *Makes 8 to 10 servings*

Serving Suggestion: Place slices of toasted Italian bread in bottom of individual soup bowls. Drizzle with olive oil. Pour soup over bread and serve.

Tortilla Soup

        2 cans (14½ ounces each) chicken broth
        1 can (14½ ounces) diced tomatoes with jalapeño peppers, undrained
        2 cups chopped carrots
        2 cups frozen whole kernel corn
    1½ cups chopped onion
        1 can (8 ounces) tomato sauce
        1 tablespoon chili powder
        1 teaspoon ground cumin
        ¼ teaspoon garlic powder
        2 cups chopped cooked chicken (optional)
          Shredded Monterey Jack cheese
          Tortilla chips, broken

1. Combine broth, tomatoes with juice, carrots, corn, onion, tomato sauce, chili powder, cumin and garlic powder in slow cooker. Cover; cook on LOW 6 to 8 hours.

2. Stir in chicken, if desired. Ladle into bowls. Top each serving with cheese and tortilla chips.

Makes 6 servings

SLOW COOKING SECRET

One advantage of slow cooking is that you can put it together and forget it.

Chili with Chocolate

  1 pound ground beef
  1 medium onion, chopped
  3 cloves garlic, minced, divided
  1 can (28 ounces) diced tomatoes, undrained
  1 can (15 ounces) chili beans
  1½ tablespoons chili powder
  1 tablespoon grated semisweet baking chocolate
  1½ teaspoons cumin
  ½ teaspoon salt
  ½ teaspoon black pepper
  ½ teaspoon hot pepper sauce

1. Brown ground beef, onion and 1 clove garlic in large nonstick skillet over medium-low heat. Drain off fat.

2. Place meat mixture into slow cooker. Add remaining ingredients including 2 cloves garlic; mix well. Cover; cook on LOW 5 to 6 hours. Garnish as desired.   *Makes 4 servings*

Chili with Chocolate

Butternut Squash-Apple Soup

**3 packages (12 ounces each) frozen cooked winter squash, thawed and drained
or about 4½ cups mashed cooked butternut squash**
2 cans (14½ ounces each) chicken broth (3 to 4 cups)
1 medium Golden Delicious apple, peeled and chopped
2 tablespoons minced onion
1 tablespoon packed light brown sugar
1 teaspoon minced fresh sage *or* ½ teaspoon ground sage
¼ teaspoon ground ginger
½ cup heavy cream or half-and-half

1. Combine all ingredients except cream in slow cooker. Cover; cook on HIGH about 3 hours or on LOW about 6 hours.

2. Purée soup in blender, food processor or with electric mixer. Return to slow cooker; keep warm. Stir in cream just before serving.   *Makes 6 to 8 servings*

Note: For thicker soup, use 3 cups chicken broth.

Butternut Squash-Apple Soup

Campfire Sausage and Potato Soup

1 can (15½ ounces) dark kidney beans, rinsed and drained
1 can (14½ ounces) diced tomatoes, undrained
1 can (10½ ounces) condensed beef broth
8 ounces kielbasa sausage, cut lengthwise into halves, then crosswise into
    ½-inch pieces
1 large baking potato, cut into ½-inch cubes
1 medium onion, diced
1 medium green bell pepper, diced
1 teaspoon dried oregano leaves
½ teaspoon sugar
1 to 2 teaspoons ground cumin

Combine all ingredients except cumin in slow cooker. Cover; cook on LOW 8 hours or on HIGH 4 hours. Stir in cumin; serve.

Makes 6 to 7 servings

Campfire Sausage and Potato Soup

Russian Borscht

          4 cups thinly sliced green cabbage
    1½ pounds fresh beets, shredded
          5 small carrots, peeled, cut lengthwise into halves, then cut into 1-inch pieces
          1 parsnip, peeled, cut lengthwise into halves, then cut into 1-inch pieces
          1 cup chopped onion
          4 cloves garlic, minced
          1 pound lean beef stew meat, cut into ½-inch cubes
          1 can (14½ ounces) diced tomatoes, undrained
          3 cans (14½ ounces each) reduced-sodium beef broth
    ¼ cup lemon juice
          1 tablespoon sugar
          1 teaspoon black pepper
          Sour cream (optional)
          Fresh parsley (optional)

1. Layer ingredients in slow cooker in the following order: cabbage, beets, carrots, parsnip, onion, garlic, beef, tomatoes with juice, broth, lemon juice, sugar and pepper. Cover; cook on LOW 7 to 9 hours or until vegetables are crisp-tender.

2. Season with additional lemon juice and sugar, if desired. Dollop with sour cream and garnish with parsley, if desired.   *Makes 12 servings*

Russian Borscht

Three-Bean Turkey Chili

1 pound ground turkey
1 small onion, chopped
1 can (28 ounces) diced tomatoes, undrained
1 can (14½ ounces) chick-peas, rinsed and drained
1 can (14½ ounces) kidney beans, rinsed and drained
1 can (14½ ounces) black beans, rinsed and drained
1 can (8 ounces) tomato sauce
1 can (4 ounces) diced mild green chilies
1 to 2 tablespoons chili powder

1. Cook turkey and onion in medium skillet over medium-high heat, stirring to break up meat until turkey is no longer pink. Drain; place turkey mixture into slow cooker.

2. Add all remaining ingredients and mix well. Cover; cook on HIGH 6 to 8 hours.

Makes 6 to 8 servings

Three-Bean Turkey Chili

French Onion Soup

4 tablespoons butter, divided
3 pounds yellow onions, sliced
1 tablespoon sugar
2 to 3 tablespoons dry white wine or water
2 quarts (8 cups) beef broth
8 to 16 slices French bread
½ cup shredded Gruyère or Swiss cheese

1. Melt butter in large skillet over medium to low heat. Add onions; cover and cook just until onions are limp and transparent, but not browned, about 10 minutes.

2. Remove cover. Sprinkle sugar over onions. Cook, stirring, until onions are caramelized, 8 to 10 minutes. Scrape onions and any browned bits into slow cooker. If necessary, deglaze pan by adding wine to pan, returning to heat, bringing to a boil, and scraping up any browned bits with a wooden spoon; add to slow cooker with onions. Stir in broth. Cover; cook on HIGH 6 hours or on LOW 8 hours.

3. Preheat broiler. To serve, ladle soup into individual soup bowls; top with 1 or 2 slices bread and about 1 tablespoon cheese. Place under broiler until cheese is melted and bubbly.

Makes 8 servings

Variation: Substitute 2 cups dry white wine for 2 cups of the beef broth.

Ham and Navy Bean Soup

        8 ounces dried navy beans, rinsed and drained
        6 cups water
        1 ham bone
        1 medium yellow onion, chopped
        2 celery stalks, finely chopped
        2 bay leaves
     1½ teaspoons dried tarragon leaves
     1½ teaspoons salt
        ¼ teaspoon black pepper

1. Place beans in large bowl; cover completely with water. Soak 6 to 8 hours or overnight. Drain beans; discard water.

2. Combine beans, 6 cups water, ham bone, onion, celery, bay leaves and tarragon in slow cooker. Cover; cook on LOW 8 hours or on HIGH 4 hours. Discard ham bone and bay leaves; stir in salt and pepper. *Makes 8 servings*

Quick-N-Easy Chili

        1 teaspoon vegetable oil
        1 pound extra-lean ground beef
        1 envelope (1 ounce) chili seasoning mix
        1 medium onion, chopped
        1 can (46 ounces) tomato juice
        1 large can (28 ounces) diced tomatoes, undrained
        1 can (15 ounces) light red kidney beans, rinsed and drained
        1 can (4 ounces) sliced mushrooms, drained

1. Heat oil in large skillet over medium-low heat. Cook and stir beef and onion until beef is browned. Drain excess fat.

2. Place beef mixture in slow cooker. Add chili seasoning mix; stir. Add tomato juice, tomatoes, kidney beans and mushrooms; mix well. Cover; cook on HIGH. When all ingredients are heated through, reduce heat to LOW; cook 6 to 8 hours. *Makes 4 servings*

Cook-Ahead Beef Meals

Meatballs in Burgundy Sauce

  60 frozen fully-cooked meatballs
   3 cups chopped onions
1½ cups water
   1 cup red wine
   2 packages (about 8 ounces) beef gravy mix
 ¼ cup ketchup
   1 tablespoon dried oregano leaves
    Hot cooked noodles

1. Combine all ingredients except noodles in slow cooker; stir to blend. Cover; cook on HIGH 5 hours.

2. Serve with noodles. *Makes 6 to 8 servings*

Serving Suggestion: Serve as an appetizer with cocktail picks and remaining sauce as a dip.

Meatballs in Burgundy Sauce

Fiery Chile Beef

    1 flank steak (about 1 to 1½ pounds)
    1 can (28 ounces) diced tomatoes, undrained
    1 can (15 ounces) pinto beans, rinsed and drained
    1 medium onion, chopped
    2 cloves garlic, minced
    ½ teaspoon salt
    ½ teaspoon ground cumin
    ¼ teaspoon black pepper
    1 canned chipotle chile pepper in adobo sauce
    1 teaspoon adobo sauce from canned chile pepper
      Flour tortillas

1. Cut flank steak into 6 evenly-sized pieces. Place flank steak, tomatoes with juice, beans, onion, garlic, salt, cumin and black pepper into slow cooker.

2. Dice chile pepper. Add pepper and adobo sauce to slow cooker; mix well. Cover; cook on LOW 7 to 8 hours. Serve with tortillas.   *Makes 6 servings*

Note: Chipotle chile peppers are dried, smoked jalapeño peppers with a very hot yet smoky and sweet flavor. They can be found dried, pickled and canned in adobo sauce.

Slow Cooker Round Steak with Gravy

    1 pound beef round steak
    1 can (10¾ ounces) condensed cream of chicken or cream of mushroom soup
    ½ cup water
    1 package (1 ounce) dry onion soup mix

Combine all ingredients in slow cooker. Cover; cook on LOW 8 hours or on HIGH 6 hours.
                                                                    Makes 4 servings

Fiery Chile Beef

Picadillo

1 pound ground beef
1 small onion, chopped
1 clove garlic, minced
1 can (14½ ounces) diced tomatoes, undrained
¼ cup golden raisins
1 tablespoon chili powder
1 tablespoon cider vinegar
½ teaspoon ground cumin
½ teaspoon dried oregano leaves
½ teaspoon ground cinnamon
¼ teaspoon red pepper flakes
1 teaspoon salt
¼ cup slivered almonds (optional)

1. Cook ground beef, onion and garlic in large nonstick skillet over medium heat until beef is no longer pink; drain. Place mixture into slow cooker.

2. Add tomatoes, raisins, chili powder, vinegar, cumin, oregano, cinnamon and pepper flakes to slow cooker. Cover; cook on LOW 6 to 7 hours. Stir in salt. Garnish with almonds, if desired.

Makes 4 servings

SLOW COOKING SECRET

Browning meats before adding to the slow cooker helps reduce the fat. Just remember to drain off the fat in the skillet before transferring meat to the slow cooker.

Braciola

1 can (28 ounces) tomato sauce
2½ teaspoons dried oregano leaves, divided
1¼ teaspoons dried basil leaves, divided
1 teaspoon salt
½ pound bulk hot Italian sausage
½ cup chopped onion
¼ cup grated Parmesan cheese
2 cloves garlic, minced
1 tablespoon dried parsley flakes
2½ pounds flank steak

1. Combine tomato sauce, 2 teaspoons oregano, 1 teaspoon basil and salt in medium bowl; set aside.

2. Cook sausage in large nonstick skillet over medium-high heat until no longer pink stirring to separate; drain well. Combine sausage, onion, cheese, garlic, parsley, remaining ½ teaspoon oregano and ¼ teaspoon basil in medium bowl; set aside.

3. Place steak on countertop between two pieces waxed paper. Pound with meat mallet until steak is ⅛ to ¼ inch thick. Cut steak into about 3-inch wide strips.

4. Spoon sausage mixture evenly onto each strip. Roll up jelly-roll style, securing meat with toothpicks. Place each roll in slow cooker. Pour reserved tomato sauce mixture over meat. Cover; cook on LOW 6 to 8 hours.

5. Cut each roll into slices. Arrange slices on dinner plates. Top with hot tomato sauce.

Makes 6 to 8 servings

Spicy Italian Beef

1 boneless beef chuck roast (3 to 4 pounds)
1 jar (12 ounces) pepperoncini (mild salad peppers)
1 can (14½ ounces) beef broth
1 can (12 ounces) beer
1 package (1 ounce) Italian salad dressing mix
1 loaf French bread, thickly sliced
10 slices provolone cheese (optional)

1. Trim visible fat from roast. Cut roast, if necessary, to fit into slow cooker, leaving meat in as many large pieces as possible.

2. Drain peppers; pull off stem ends. Add to slow cooker along with broth, beer and dressing mix; do not stir. Cover; cook on low 8 to 10 hours.

3. Remove meat from sauce; shred with 2 forks. Return shredded meat to slow cooker; mix well.

4. Serve on French bread slice, topped with cheese, if desired. Add sauce and peppers as desired.

Makes 8 to 10 servings

Spicy Italian Beef

Italian-Style Pot Roast

        2 teaspoons minced garlic
        1 teaspoon salt
        1 teaspoon dried basil leaves
        1 teaspoon dried oregano leaves
        ¼ teaspoon red pepper flakes
    2½ to 3 pounds beef bottom round rump or chuck shoulder roast
        1 large onion, quartered and thinly sliced
    1½ cups prepared tomato basil or marinara spaghetti sauce
        2 cans (16 ounces each) cannellini or Great Northern beans, drained
        ¼ cup shredded fresh basil or chopped Italian parsley

1. Combine garlic, salt, basil, oregano and pepper flakes in small bowl; rub over roast.

2. Place ½ onion slices into slow cooker. Cut roast in half to fit into slow cooker. Place one half of roast over onion slices; top with remaining onion slices and other half of roast. Pour spaghetti sauce over roast. Cover; cook on LOW 8 to 9 hours or until roast is fork tender.

3. Remove roast from cooking liquid; tent with foil.

4. Let liquid in slow cooker stand 5 minutes to allow fat to rise. Skim off fat.

5. Stir beans into liquid. Cover; cook on HIGH 10 to 15 minutes or until beans are hot. Carve roast across the grain into thin slices. Serve with bean mixture and garnish with basil.

Makes 6 to 8 servings

Italian-Style Pot Roast

Slow Cooker Steak Fajitas

  1 pound beef flank steak, cut across the grain into thin strips
  1 medium onion, cut into strips
  ½ cup medium salsa
  2 tablespoons fresh lime juice
  2 tablespoons chopped fresh cilantro
  2 cloves garlic, minced
  1 tablespoon chili powder
  1 teaspoon ground cumin
  ½ teaspoon salt
  1 small green bell pepper, cut into strips
  1 small red bell pepper, cut into strips
  Flour tortillas, warmed
  Additional salsa (optional)

1. Combine all ingredients except bell peppers, tortillas and additional salsa in slow cooker. Cover; cook on LOW 5 to 6 hours. Add bell peppers. Cover; cook on LOW 1 hour.

2. Serve with flour tortillas and additional salsa, if desired.   *Makes 4 servings*

Slow Cooker Steak Fajitas

Round Steak

  1 round steak (1½ pounds), trimmed and cut into 4 equal-size pieces
¼ cup all-purpose flour
  1 teaspoon black pepper
½ teaspoon salt
  1 tablespoon vegetable oil
  1 can (10¾ ounces) condensed cream of mushroom soup
¾ cup water
  1 medium onion, quartered
  1 can (4 ounces) sliced mushrooms, drained
¼ cup milk
  1 package (1 ounce) dry onion soup mix
    Salt and black pepper
    Ground sage
    Dried thyme leaves
  1 bay leaf

1. Place steaks in large plastic bag food storage bag. Close bag and pound with mallet to tenderize. Combine flour, black pepper and salt in small bowl; add to bag with steaks. Shake to coat meat evenly.

2. Heat oil in large nonstick skillet. Remove steaks from bag; shake off excess flour. Add steaks to skillet; brown on both sides.

3. Transfer steaks with pan juices, mushroom soup, water, onion, mushrooms, milk, soup mix seasonings to taste and bay leaf to slow cooker. Cover; cook on LOW 5 to 6 hours or until steaks are tender. Remove bay leaf before serving. *Makes 4 servings*

Round Steak

Slow-Cooked Smothered Steak

⅓ cup all-purpose flour
1 teaspoon garlic salt
½ teaspoon black pepper
1½ pounds beef chuck or round steak, cut into strips
1 large onion, sliced
1 to 2 medium green bell peppers, cut into strips
1 can (4 ounces) sliced mushrooms, drained
¼ cup teriyaki sauce
1 package (10 ounces) frozen French-style green beans

1. Combine flour, garlic salt and black pepper in medium bowl. Add steak strips, tossing to coat with flour mixture. Place into slow cooker.

2. Layer remaining ingredients in slow cooker. Cover; cook on HIGH 1 hour. Reduce heat to LOW; cook on LOW 8 hours or on HIGH 5 hours.

Makes 6 servings

SLOW COOKING SECRET

Spinning the cover until the condensation falls off allows you to see inside the slow cooker without removing the lid, which delays the cooking time.

Mama Mia Spaghetti Sauce

   1 tablespoon olive oil
   1 package (8 ounces) sliced mushrooms
  ½ cup finely chopped carrots
   1 clove garlic, minced
   1 shallot, minced
   1 pound lean ground beef
   2 cups canned or fresh crushed tomatoes
  ½ cup dry red wine or beef broth
   2 tablespoons tomato paste
   1 teaspoon salt
   1 teaspoon dried oregano leaves
  ½ teaspoon dried basil leaves
  ¼ teaspoon black pepper
   4 cups cooked spaghetti
    Grated Parmesan cheese (optional)

1. Heat oil in large skillet over medium-high heat until hot. Add mushrooms, carrots, garlic and shallot to skillet. Cook and stir 5 minutes. Place vegetables in slow cooker.

2. Add ground beef to skillet; brown, stirring to break up meat. Drain fat. Place beef into slow cooker.

3. Add tomatoes, wine, tomato paste, salt, oregano, basil and pepper. Cover; cook on HIGH 3 to 4 hours. Serve sauce with cooked spaghetti. Sprinkle with Parmesan cheese, if desired.

Makes 5 servings

Smothered Beef Patties

   Worcestershire sauce
   Garlic powder
   Salt
   Black pepper
 1 can (14½ ounces) Mexican-style diced tomatoes with chilies, undrained, divided
 8 frozen beef patties, unthawed
 1 onion, cut into 8 slices

Sprinkle bottom of slow cooker with small amount of Worcestershire sauce, garlic powder, salt, pepper and 2 tablespoons tomatoes. Place 1 frozen beef patty on seasonings. Season top of patty with more of same seasonings. Place slice of onion on top each patty. Repeat layers. Cover; cook on LOW 8 hours. *Makes 8 servings*

Serving Suggestion: Serve with mashed potatoes and Caesar salad. Also delicious with steamed rice.

Easy Beef Stew

 1½ to 2 pounds beef for stew
   4 medium potatoes, cubed
   4 carrots, cut into 1½-inch pieces *or* 4 cups baby carrots
   1 medium onion, cut into 8 wedges
   2 cans (8 ounces each) tomato sauce
   1 teaspoon salt
 ½ teaspoon black pepper

Combine all ingredients in slow cooker. Cover; cook on LOW 8 to 10 hours or until vegetables are tender. *Makes 6 to 8 servings*

Smothered Beef Patty

Slow-Cooked Korean Beef Short Ribs

4 to 4½ pounds beef short ribs
¼ cup chopped green onions with tops
¼ cup tamari or soy sauce
¼ cup beef broth or water
1 tablespoon brown sugar
2 teaspoons minced fresh ginger
2 teaspoons minced garlic
½ teaspoon black pepper
2 teaspoons Asian sesame oil
Hot cooked rice or linguini pasta
2 teaspoons sesame seeds, toasted

1. Place ribs in slow cooker. Combine green onions, soy sauce, broth, brown sugar, ginger, garlic and pepper in medium bowl; mix well and pour over ribs. Cover; cook on LOW 7 to 8 hours or until ribs are fork tender.

2. Remove ribs from cooking liquid, cool slightly. Trim excess fat. Cut rib meat into bite-sized pieces discarding bones and fat.

3. Let cooking liquid stand 5 minutes to allow fat to rise. Skim off fat.

4. Stir sesame oil into liquid. Return beef to slow cooker. Cover; cook on LOW 15 to 30 minutes or until mixture is hot. Serve with rice or pasta; garnish with sesame seeds.

Makes 6 servings

Variation: 3 pounds boneless short ribs may be substituted for beef short ribs.

Beef with Green Chilies

¼ **cup plus 1 tablespoon all-purpose flour**
½ **teaspoon salt**
¼ **teaspoon black pepper**
1 **pound beef for stew**
1 **tablespoon vegetable oil**
2 **cloves garlic, minced**
1 **cup beef broth**
1 **can (7 ounces) diced mild green chilies, drained**
½ **teaspoon dried oregano leaves**
2 **tablespoons water**
   Hot cooked rice (optional)
   Diced tomato (optional)

1. Combine ¼ cup flour, salt and pepper in resealable plastic food storage bag. Add beef; shake to coat beef. Heat oil in large skillet over medium-high heat. Add beef and garlic. Brown beef on all sides. Place beef mixture into slow cooker. Add broth to skillet scraping up any browned bits. Pour broth mixture into slow cooker. Add chilies and oregano.

2. Cover; cook on LOW 7 to 8 hours. For thicker sauce, combine remaining 1 tablespoon flour and water in small bowl stirring until mixture is smooth. Stir mixture into slow cooker; mix well. Cover and cook until thickened.

3. Serve with rice and garnish with diced tomato, if desired.   *Makes 4 servings*

Variation: Use two cans of chilies for a slightly hotter taste.

Peppered Beef Tips

    1 pound beef sirloin tips
    2 cloves garlic, minced
      Black pepper
    1 can (10¾ ounces) condensed French onion soup
    1 can (10¾ ounces) condensed cream of mushroom soup

Place beef tips in slow cooker. Sprinkle with garlic and pepper. Pour soups over beef. Cover; cook on LOW 8 to 10 hours. *Makes 2 to 3 servings*

Serving Suggestion: Serve over cooked noodles or rice.

Beef with Mushroom and Red Wine Gravy

    1½ pounds well-trimmed beef stew meat, cut into 1-inch cubes
    2 medium onions, cut into ½-inch wedges
    1 package (8 ounces) sliced baby button, cremini or other fresh mushrooms
    1 package (about 1 ounce) dry beefy onion soup mix
    3 tablespoons cornstarch
    ⅛ teaspoon salt
    ⅛ teaspoon black pepper
    1½ cups dry red wine

Place beef, onions and mushrooms into slow cooker. Sprinkle with soup mix, cornstarch, salt and pepper. Pour wine over all. Cover; cook on LOW 10 to 12 hours or on HIGH 5 to 6 hours. *Makes 6 servings*

Peppered Beef Tips

Autumn Delight

    4 to 6 beef cubed steaks
    Olive oil
    2 to 3 cans (10¾ ounces each) condensed cream of mushroom soup
    1 to 1½ cups water
    1 package (1 ounce) dry onion or mushroom soup mix

1. Lightly brown cubed steaks in oil in large nonstick skillet over medium heat.

2. Place steaks into slow cooker. Add soup, water (½ cup water per can of soup) and soup mix; stir. Cover; cook on LOW 4 to 6 hours.   *Makes 4 to 6 servings*

Best Ever Slow Cooker Pot Roast

    1 beef chuck shoulder roast (3 to 4 pounds)
    1 can (10 ounces) beef gravy
    ½ cup dry red wine
    1 package (1 ounce) au jus mix
    ½ package Italian salad dressing mix
    2 tablespoons all-purpose flour
    ½ cup cold water

1. Place roast in slow cooker. Combine gravy, wine, au jus mix and salad dressing mix into medium bowl. Pour mixture over meat. Cover; cook on LOW 8 to 10 hours.

2. Remove roast to plate; cover with foil to keep warm. Turn slow cooker to HIGH. Mix flour into water until smooth. Stir into juices in slow cooker. Cook 15 minutes or until thickened.

Makes 8 servings

Autumn Delight

Slow-Cooked Pot Roast

1 tablespoon vegetable oil
1 beef brisket (3 to 4 pounds)
1 tablespoon garlic powder, divided
1 tablespoon salt, divided
1 tablespoon black pepper, divided
1 teaspoon paprika, divided
5 to 6 new potatoes, cut into quarters
4 to 5 medium onions, sliced
1 pound baby carrots
1 can (14½ ounces) beef broth

1. Heat 1 tablespoon oil on HIGH in slow cooker. Brown brisket on all sides. Remove brisket to plate. Season with 1½ teaspoons garlic powder, 1½ teaspoons salt, 1½ teaspoons pepper and ½ teaspoon paprika; set aside.

2. Season potatoes with remaining 1½ teaspoons garlic powder, 1½ teaspoons salt, 1½ teaspoons pepper and ½ teaspoon paprika. Add potatoes and onions to slow cooker. Cook on HIGH, stirring occasionally, until browned.

3. Return brisket to slow cooker. Add carrots and broth. Cover; cook on HIGH 4 to 5 hours or on LOW 8 to 10 hours or until meat is tender. *Makes 6 to 8 servings*

Serving Suggestion: Arrange potatoes and carrots around the sliced beef. Spoon on broth to keep the meat moist.

Harvest Beef Stew

   1 tablespoon olive oil
1½ pounds beef for stew
   1 can (28 ounces) stewed tomatoes, undrained
   6 carrots, cut into 1-inch pieces
   3 medium potatoes, cut into 1-inch pieces
   3 ribs celery, chopped (about 1 cup)
   1 medium onion, sliced
   1 cup apple juice
   2 tablespoons dried parsley flakes
   1 tablespoon dried basil leaves
   2 teaspoons salt
   1 clove garlic, minced
  ½ teaspoon black pepper
   2 bay leaves
  ¼ cup all-purpose flour (optional)
  ½ cup warm water (optional)

1. Heat oil in large skillet over medium-low heat. Brown stew meat on all sides. Drain excess fat.

2. Place browned meat and all remaining ingredients except flour and water into slow cooker. Mix well. Cover; cook on HIGH 6 to 7 hours.

3. Before serving, thicken gravy, if desired. Combine flour and warm water in small bowl, stirring well until all lumps are gone. Add mixture to liquid in slow cooker; mix well. Cook 10 to 20 minutes or until sauce thickens. Remove and discard bay leaves before serving.

Makes 6 servings

Beef and Vegetables in Rich Burgundy Sauce

1 package (8 ounces) sliced mushrooms
1 package (8 ounces) baby carrots
1 medium green bell pepper, cut into thin strips
1 boneless beef chuck roast (2½ pounds)
1 can (10½ ounces) condensed golden mushroom soup
¼ cup dry red wine or beef broth
1 tablespoon Worcestershire sauce
1 package (1 ounce) dry onion soup mix
¼ teaspoon black pepper
3 tablespoons cornstarch
2 tablespoons water
4 cups hot cooked noodles
Chopped fresh parsley (optional)

1. Place mushrooms, carrots and bell pepper in slow cooker. Place roast on top of vegetables. Combine mushroom soup, wine, Worcestershire sauce, soup mix and black pepper in medium bowl; mix well. Pour soup mixture over roast. Cover; cook on LOW 8 to 10 hours.

2. Transfer roast to cutting board; cover with foil. Let stand 10 to 15 minutes before slicing.

3. Blend cornstarch and water until smooth. Turn slow cooker to HIGH. Stir cornstarch mixture into vegetable mixture; cook 10 minutes or until thickened. Serve beef and vegetables with sauce over cooked noodles. Garnish with parsley, if desired. *Makes 6 to 8 servings*

Beef and Vegetables in Rich Burgundy Sauce

Saucy Braised Beef

2 pounds beef top round, trimmed and cut into bite-size pieces
1 tablespoon mixed dried herbs
  Salt
  Black pepper
2 tablespoons oil
2 cups baby carrots
1 large yellow onion, thinly sliced
1 medium zucchini, cut into 1-inch slices
2 tablespoons minced garlic
1 teaspoon dried oregano leaves
1 can (8 ounces) tomato sauce
1 can (6 ounces) tomato paste
½ cup molasses
2 tablespoons red wine vinegar
2 teaspoons hot pepper sauce

1. Lightly season beef with mixed herbs, salt and pepper to taste. Heat oil in Dutch oven or large skillet over medium-low heat. Brown meat on all sides. Drain excess fat. Place beef into slow cooker.

2. Add carrots, onion, zucchini, garlic and oregano to Dutch oven. Cook over medium-low heat 4 to 5 minutes or until onion is tender, stirring occasionally. Add vegetable mixture and remaining ingredients to slow cooker; mix well.

3. Cover; cook on LOW 8 to 10 hours.

Makes 4 to 6 servings

Beef with Apples and Sweet Potatoes

2 pounds boneless beef chuck shoulder roast
1 can (40 ounces) sweet potatoes, drained
2 small onions, sliced
2 apples, cored and sliced
½ cup beef broth
2 cloves garlic, minced
1 teaspoon salt
1 teaspoon dried thyme leaves, divided
¾ teaspoon black pepper, divided
1 tablespoon cornstarch
¼ teaspoon ground cinnamon
2 tablespoons cold water

1. Trim fat from beef and cut into 2-inch pieces. Place beef, sweet potatoes, onions, apples, beef broth, garlic, salt, ½ teaspoon thyme and ½ teaspoon pepper in slow cooker. Cover; cook on LOW 8 to 9 hours.

2. Transfer beef, sweet potatoes and apples to platter; keep warm. Let liquid stand 5 minutes to allow fat to rise. Skim off fat.

3. Combine cornstarch, remaining ½ teaspoon thyme, ¼ teaspoon pepper, cinnamon and water; stir into cooking liquid. Cook 15 minutes or until juices are thickened. Serve sauce with beef, sweet potatoes and apples.

Makes 6 servings

Beef Roll Ups

    1 beef round steak (1½ pounds), ½ inch thick
    4 slices bacon
    ½ cup diced green bell pepper
    ¼ cup diced onion
    ¼ cup diced celery
    1 can (10 ounces) beef gravy

1. Cut steak into 4 pieces. Place 1 bacon slice on each piece.

2. Combine bell pepper, onion, and celery in medium bowl. Place about ¼ cup mixture on each piece of meat. Roll up meat jelly-roll style; secure with wooden toothpicks.

3. Place beef rolls in slow cooker. Pour gravy evenly over steaks. Cover; cook on LOW 8 to 10 hours. Skim off fat before serving. *Makes 4 servings*

Serving Suggestion: Serve with mashed potatoes or over rice.

Easy Beef Burgundy

    1½ pounds beef round steak, cut into 1-inch pieces or beef for stew
    1 can (10¾ ounces) condensed cream of mushroom soup
    1 cup red wine
    1 small onion, chopped
    1 can (4 ounces) sliced mushrooms, drained
    1 package (1 ounce) dry onion soup mix
    1 tablespoon minced garlic

Combine all ingredients in slow cooker. Cover; cook on LOW 6 to 8 hours or until beef is tender. *Makes 4 to 6 servings*

Serving Suggestion: Serve over noodles, rice or mashed potatoes.

Beef Roll Up

Corned Beef and Cabbage

1 head cabbage (1½ pounds), cut into 6 wedges
4 ounces baby carrots
1 corned beef (3 pounds) with seasoning packet*
1 quart (4 cups) water
⅓ cup prepared mustard (optional)
⅓ cup honey (optional)

*If seasoning packet is not perforated, poke several small holes with tip of paring knife.

1. Place cabbage in slow cooker; top with carrots.

2. Place seasoning packet on top of vegetables. Place corned beef, fat side up, over seasoning packet and vegetables. Add water. Cover; cook on LOW 10 hours.

3. Discard seasoning packet. Just before serving, combine mustard and honey in small bowl. Use as dipping sauce, if desired.   *Makes 6 servings*

Beef Stew

1 pound potatoes, cut into 1-inch cubes
1 pound baby carrots
1 large onion, chopped *or* 1 package (10 ounces) frozen peas and pearl onions
2 pounds beef for stew
1 can (10¾ ounces) condensed cream of mushroom soup
1 can (10¾ ounces) condensed French onion soup

Place potatoes in bottom of slow cooker; top with baby carrots and onion. Place meat on top. Pour soups over top. Cover; cook on LOW 8 to 10 hours.   *Makes 8 servings*

Corned Beef and Cabbage

Beef and Noodles

    1 tablespoon vegetable oil
    1 beef chuck shoulder roast (3 pounds)
    1 can (10¾ ounces) condensed cream of mushroom or cream of potato soup
    1 cup cooking sherry
    1 cup water
    1 package (1 ounce) dry onion soup mix
    1 package (12 ounces) egg noodles, cooked according to package directions

1. Heat oil in large skillet over medium-low heat. Brown roast on all sides. Drain excess fat.

2. Place meat and remaining ingredients except noodles into slow cooker. Cover; cook on LOW 8 hours, stirring once or twice during cooking.

3. Serve roast over noodles.

Makes 8 servings

So Simple Supper!

    1 beef chuck shoulder roast (3 to 4 pounds)
    1 package (1 ounce) mushroom gravy mix
    1 package (1 ounce) dry onion gravy mix
    1 package (1 ounce) au jus gravy mix
    3 cups water
      Assorted vegetables (potatoes, carrots, onions, celery, etc.)

1. Place roast in slow cooker. Combine gravy mixes and water in large bowl . Pour gravy mixture over roast. Cover; cook on LOW 4 hours.

2. Add vegetables and cook 2 more hours or until meat and vegetables are tender.

Makes 8 servings

Ranch Stew

- 2 pounds beef for stew
- 6 medium potatoes, diced
- 2 cups sliced carrots
- 2 medium onions, chopped
- 1 medium green bell pepper, chopped (optional)
- 1 cup diced celery (optional)
- 1 can (10¾ ounces) condensed tomato soup
- 1 soup can water
- 2 tablespoons tapioca
- 1 tablespoon Worcestershire sauce
- 2 teaspoons salt
- 1 teaspoon soy sauce
- ¼ teaspoon black pepper
- 1 bay leaf

Combine all ingredients in slow cooker. Cover; cook on LOW 10 to 12 hours or until tender. Remove and discard bay leaf before serving. *Makes 6 servings*

SLOW COOKING SECRET

Vegetables such as potatoes and carrots can sometimes take longer to cook in a slow cooker than the meat. Place evenly cut vegetables on the bottom or along the sides of the slow cooker when possible.

Slow Cooker Stuffed Peppers

1 package (7 ounces) Spanish rice mix
1 pound ground beef
½ cup diced celery
1 small onion, chopped
1 egg
4 medium green bell peppers, halved lengthwise, cored and seeded
1 can (28 ounces) whole peeled tomatoes, undrained
1 can (10¾ ounces) condensed tomato soup
1 cup water

1. Set aside seasoning packet from rice. Combine beef, rice mix, celery, onion and egg in large bowl. Divide meat mixture evenly among pepper halves.

2. Pour tomatoes with juice into slow cooker. Arrange filled pepper halves on top of tomatoes. Combine tomato soup, water and reserved rice mix seasoning packet in large bowl. Pour over peppers. Cover; cook on LOW 8 to 10 hours. *Makes 4 servings*

Slow Cooker Beef & Noodles

1 can (10½ ounces) condensed French onion soup
1 can (10¾ ounces) condensed cream of mushroom soup
1 to 1½ pounds beef for stew
1 bag (12 ounces) extra-wide egg noodles, cooked

1. Combine soups and meat in slow cooker; stir. Cover; cook on LOW 8 to 10 hours.

2. Serve with prepared noodles. *Makes 4 to 6 servings*

Slow Cooker Stuffed Peppers

Country-Style Steak

    4 to 6 beef cubed steaks
    All-purpose flour
    1 tablespoon vegetable oil
    1 package (1 ounce) dry onion soup mix
    1 package (1 ounce) brown gravy mix
    Water

1. Dust steaks with flour. Heat oil in large skillet over medium-low heat. Brown steaks on both sides. Drain excess fat.

2. Place steaks in slow cooker. Add soup and gravy mixes and enough water to cover meat. Cover; cook on LOW 6 to 8 hours. *Makes 4 to 6 servings*

Serving Suggestion: Serve with mashed potatoes.

Slow Cooker Beef Stroganoff

    1½ to 2 pounds beef for stew
    1 can (10¾ ounces) condensed cream of mushroom soup
    1 can (4 ounces) sliced mushrooms, drained
    1 package (1 ounce) dry onion soup mix

Combine meat, mushroom soup, mushrooms and onion soup mix in slow cooker. Cover; cook on LOW 6 to 8 hours. *Makes 4 to 6 servings*

Serving Suggestion: Serve with hot cooked rice or noodles.

Spaghetti Sauce

       1 tablespoon olive oil
  1½ pounds ground beef
       1 medium onion, chopped
       1 medium green bell pepper, diced
       2 cans (28 ounces each) crushed tomatoes, undrained
       1 can (15 ounces) beef broth
       1 can (8 ounces) tomato sauce
       1 can (6 ounces) tomato paste (or more to taste)
  ½ cup grated Parmesan cheese
       1 tablespoon brown sugar
       2 teaspoons garlic powder
       1 teaspoon dried oregano leaves
       1 teaspoon dried basil leaves

1. Heat oil in large skillet over medium-low heat. Add ground beef, onion and bell pepper. Cook, stirring frequently, until meat is no longer pink and onion is tender. Drain excess fat.

2. Place meat mixture into slow cooker. Add remaining ingredients; stir thoroughly. Cover; cook on LOW 6 to 8 hours.   *Makes 6 servings*

SLOW COOKING SECRET

Jazz up the flavor of slow cooker dishes by adding a small amount of snipped fresh herbs or freshly ground pepper just before serving.

Mushroom-Beef Stew

  1 pound beef stew meat
  1 can (10¾ ounces) condensed cream of mushroom soup
  2 cans (4 ounces each) sliced mushrooms, drained
  1 package (1 ounce) dry onion soup mix

Combine all ingredients in slow cooker. Cover; cook on low 8 to 10 hours.   *Makes 4 servings*

Serving Suggestion: Serve over hot cooked rice or noodles.

Slow Cooker Bean Dish

  1 pound extra-lean ground beef
  ½ pound bacon, cut into 1-inch pieces
  1 can (15 ounces) butter beans, drained
  1 can (15 ounces) garbanzo beans, drained
  1 can (15 ounces) red kidney beans, drained
  1 can (15 ounces) pork and beans
  1 cup brown sugar
  1 cup ketchup
  ½ cup diced onion
  2 tablespoons vinegar

1. Cook and stir ground beef in large skillet over medium-high heat until no longer pink. Drain excess fat.

2. Combine beef and remaining ingredients in slow cooker. Cover; cook on LOW 6 hours.

Makes 8 servings

Mushroom-Beef Stew

Beef Stew with Molasses and Raisins

⅓ cup all-purpose flour
2 teaspoons salt, divided
1½ teaspoons black pepper, divided
2 pounds boneless beef chuck roast, cut into 1½-inch pieces
5 tablespoons oil, divided
2 medium onions, sliced
1 can (28 ounces) diced tomatoes, drained
1 cup beef broth
3 tablespoons molasses
2 tablespoons cider vinegar
4 cloves garlic, minced
2 teaspoons dried thyme leaves
1 teaspoon celery salt
1 bay leaf
8 ounces baby carrots, cut in half lengthwise
2 parsnips, diced
½ cup golden raisins
Salt and black pepper

1. Combine flour, 1½ teaspoons salt and 1 teaspoon pepper in large bowl. Toss meat in flour mixture. Heat 2 tablespoons oil in large skillet or Dutch oven over medium-high heat. Add half of beef and brown on all sides. Set aside browned beef and repeat with 2 tablespoons oil and remaining beef.

2. Add remaining 1 tablespoon oil to skillet. Add onions and cook, stirring to loosen any browned bits, about 5 minutes. Add tomatoes, broth, molasses, vinegar, garlic, thyme, celery salt, bay leaf and remaining ½ teaspoon salt and ½ teaspoon pepper. Bring to a boil. Add browned beef and boil 1 minute.

3. Transfer mixture to slow cooker. Cover; cook on LOW 5 hours or on HIGH 2½ hours. Add carrots, parsnips and raisins. Continue to cook on LOW 1 to 2 hours more or until vegetables are tender. Season to taste with salt and pepper. *Makes 6 to 8 servings*

Beef Stew with Molasses and Raisins

Pot Roast

1 tablespoon vegetable oil
1 beef chuck shoulder roast (3 to 4 pounds)
6 medium potatoes, halved
2 medium onions, quartered
6 carrots, sliced
2 ribs celery, sliced
1 can (14½ ounces) diced tomatoes, undrained (optional)
Salt
Black pepper
Dried oregano leaves
Water
1½ to 2 tablespoons all-purpose flour

1. Heat oil in large skillet over medium-low heat. Add roast; brown on all sides. Drain excess fat.

2. Place roast in slow cooker. Add potatoes, onions, carrots, celery and tomatoes with juice. Season with salt, pepper and oregano to taste. Add enough water to cover bottom of slow cooker by about ½ inch. Cover; cook on LOW 8 to 10 hours.

3. Serve with cooked juices from slow cooker. To make gravy, combine juices with flour in small saucepan. Cook and stir over medium heat until thickened. *Makes 6 to 8 servings*

Barbecue Beef Cubes

   1 boneless beef roast (4 pounds), cut into cubes
   1 can (28 ounces) tomatoes, undrained
   1 can (4 ounces) tomato paste
   1 large onion, chopped
   ¼ cup firmly packed brown sugar
   ¼ cup vinegar
   2 teaspoons salt
   2 teaspoons barbecue spice mix
   2 teaspoons Worcestershire sauce
   2 cloves garlic, minced
   1 teaspoon dry mustard
   ¼ teaspoon black pepper

Place beef cubes in slow cooker. Combine remaining ingredients in large bowl; pour over meat. Cover; cook on LOW 6 to 8 hours or until tender.   *Makes 8 servings*

Serving Suggestion: Serve over rice or noodles.

SLOW COOKING SECRET

To remove fat from the liquid of cooked slow cooker dishes, first remove any solids from the liquid, let the liquid stand 5 minutes to allow the fat to surface, then skim off the fat with a large spoon.

Sauerbraten

　　　　1 boneless beef sirloin tip roast (1¼ pounds)
　　　　3 cups baby carrots
　1½ cups fresh or frozen pearl onions
　　　¼ cup raisins
　　　½ cup water
　　　½ cup red wine vinegar
　　　　1 tablespoon honey
　　　½ teaspoon salt
　　　½ teaspoon dry mustard
　　　½ teaspoon garlic-pepper seasoning
　　　¼ teaspoon ground cloves
　　　¼ cup crushed crisp gingersnap cookies (5 cookies)

1. Heat large nonstick skillet over medium heat until hot. Brown roast on all sides; set aside.

2. Place roast, carrots, onions and raisins in slow cooker. Combine water, vinegar, honey, salt, mustard, garlic-pepper seasoning and cloves in large bowl; mix well. Pour mixture over meat and vegetables.

3. Cover; cook on LOW 4 to 6 hours or until internal temperature reaches 145°F when tested with meat thermometer inserted into thickest part of roast. Transfer roast to cutting board; cover with foil. Let stand 10 to 15 minutes before slicing. Internal temperature will continue to rise 5° to 10°F during stand time.

4. Remove vegetables with slotted spoon to bowl; cover to keep warm. Stir crushed cookies into sauce mixture in slow cooker. Cover; cook on HIGH 10 to 15 minutes or until sauce thickens. Serve meat and vegetables with sauce. *Makes 5 servings*

Sauerbraten

Traci's 5-Layer Pot Roast

4 medium onions, cut into chunks, divided
1 package (16 ounces) frozen baby carrots, divided
6 celery stalks, cut into thirds, divided
   Garlic powder
   Salt
   Black pepper
   Water
1 large beef or pork roast, sliced in half horizontally
8 medium potatoes, peeled and cut into chunks
   All-purpose flour or cornstarch

1. Combine onions, carrots and celery in large bowl. Place ⅓ vegetable mixture in slow cooker. Season with garlic powder, salt and pepper to taste. Add water to cover.

2. Place bottom slice of roast on top of vegetables; season with garlic powder, salt and pepper. Top roast with ⅓ vegetables; season. Add top roast half; season. Top with remaining ⅓ vegetables; season well. Cover; cook on LOW 6 to 8 hours.

3. During last hour or two of cooking, add potatoes.

4. Serve with cooked juices from slow cooker. To make gravy, combine juices with flour in small saucepan. Cook and stir over medium heat until thickened. *Makes 8 to 10 servings*

Swiss Steak Stew

   ½ cup all-purpose flour, divided
   ½ teaspoon salt
1½ pounds boneless beef round steak, cut into bite-size pieces
     Nonstick cooking spray
   3 cups peeled and quartered red potatoes
   1 medium onion, diced
   1 can (14½ ounces) Italian-style diced tomatoes, undrained
   ¾ cup water
   1 cup corn

1. Combine ¼ cup flour and salt in large bowl. Add beef; stir to coat.

2. Coat nonstick skillet with cooking spray; heat over medium-low heat. Add beef; brown beef on all sides.

3. Layer potatoes, beef and onion in slow cooker. Combine tomatoes with juice, water and ¼ cup remaining flour in medium bowl. Pour over ingredients in slow cooker. Cover; cook on LOW 7 to 8 hours or until beef is tender.

4. Add corn. Cover; cook on LOW an additional 30 minutes.   *Makes 6 servings*

SLOW COOKING SECRET

Browning meats and poultry before cooking in the slow cooker is not necessary but can enhance flavor and appearance of the finished dish.

Slow Cooker Pepper Steak

2 tablespoons vegetable oil
3 pounds sirloin steak, cut into strips
1 heaping tablespoon minced garlic (5 to 6 cloves)
1 medium onion, chopped
½ cup reduced-sodium soy sauce
2 teaspoons sugar
1 teaspoon salt
½ teaspoon ground ginger
½ teaspoon black pepper
3 green bell peppers, cut into strips
¼ cup cold water
1 tablespoon cornstarch
   Hot cooked white rice

1. Heat oil in large skillet over medium-low heat. Brown steak strips; sprinkle with garlic.

2. Transfer meat and pan juices to slow cooker. Add onion, soy sauce, sugar, salt, ginger and black pepper; mix well. Cover; cook on LOW 6 to 8 hours or until meat is tender (up to 10 hours).

3. In final hour of cooking, add bell pepper strips. Before serving, mix together water and cornstarch; stir into slow cooker. Cook on HIGH 10 minutes or until thickened. Serve over hot rice.

Makes 6 to 8 servings

Slow Cooker Pepper Steak

Smothered Steak

1½ to 2 pounds beef cubed steaks
    All-purpose flour
1 can (10¾ ounces) condensed cream of mushroom soup
1 can (4 ounces) sliced mushrooms, drained
1 package (1 ounce) dry onion soup mix

Dust steak lightly with flour. Place in slow cooker. Combine mushroom soup, mushrooms and onion soup mix in medium bowl; pour over steak. Cover; cook on LOW 6 to 8 hours.

Makes 4 servings

Slow Cooker Hamburger Casserole

4 medium potatoes, thinly sliced
3 carrots, thinly sliced
1 can (15 ounces) green peas, drained
1 can (15 ounces) corn, drained
3 medium onions, chopped
1½ pounds extra-lean ground beef, browned and drained
    Salt
    Black pepper
1 can (10¾ ounces) condensed tomato soup
1 soup can water

Layer ingredients inside slow cooker in order listed, occasionally seasoning with salt and pepper. Cover with tomato soup and water. Cover; cook on LOW 6 to 8 hours or on HIGH 2 to 4 hours.

Makes 4 to 6 servings

Smothered Steak

Slow-Cooked Beef Brisket Dinner

1 beef brisket (4 pounds), cut in half
4 to 6 medium potatoes, cut into large chunks
6 carrots, cut into 1-inch pieces
8 ounces sliced mushrooms
½ large onion, sliced
1 rib celery, cut into 1-inch pieces
3 cubes beef bouillon
5 cloves garlic, crushed
1 teaspoon black peppercorns
2 bay leaves
Water

1. Place all ingredients in slow cooker, adding enough water to cover ingredients. Cover; cook on LOW 6 to 8 hours. Remove and discard bay leaves

2. Remove brisket to cutting board. Slice across the grain and serve with vegetables.

Makes 8 to 10 servings

Four Layer Delight

1½ teaspoons salt
1½ teaspoons dried thyme leaves
¾ teaspoon black pepper
½ pound sliced bacon, cut into 1-inch pieces
2 pounds beef round or chuck steak
3 large russet potatoes, scrubbed and sliced
2 large onions, thinly sliced

1. Combine salt, thyme and pepper in small bowl. set aside.

2. Sprinkle bacon pieces over bottom of slow cooker. Place steak on top of bacon; sprinkle with ½ seasoning mixture. Add potatoes and onions; sprinkle with remaining seasoning mixture. Cover; cook on LOW 8 hours. *Makes 4 servings*

Note: There should be plenty of liquid in the cooker, but you may need to add some water after several hours of cooking.

Excellent Tailgating Beef & Noodles

1 beef round steak (2 pounds), cubed
2 jars (10 ounces each) beef gravy
1 package (12 ounces) egg noodles, cooked according to package directions

1. Place steak cubes in slow cooker; cover with gravy. Cover; cook on LOW 8 to 10 hours.

2. To serve, spoon steak and gravy over noodles. *Makes 4 to 6 servings*

Serving Suggestion: Serve with a tossed salad for a great, easy meal.

Swiss Steak

1 beef round steak (2 pounds), cut to fit into slow cooker
All-purpose flour
Salt
Black pepper
1 onion, sliced into thick rings
1 clove garlic, minced
1 can (28 ounces) whole tomatoes, undrained
1 can (10¾ ounces) condensed tomato soup
3 medium potatoes, unpeeled, diced
1 package (16 ounces) frozen peas and carrots
1 cup sliced celery
Additional vegetables

1. Dredge steak in flour seasoned with salt and pepper. Shake off excess flour.

2. Place onion and garlic in bottom of slow cooker. Add steak and tomatoes with juice. Cover with tomato soup. Add potatoes, peas and carrots, celery and any additional vegetables. Cover; cook on HIGH 4 to 6 hours or until meat and potatoes are tender.   *Makes 8 servings*

Variation: Substitute corn or green beans for peas and carrots.

Swiss Steak

Lemon-Thyme Beef with Beans

3 pounds beef chuck roast, trimmed and cut in 2-inch pieces
2 cans (15 ounces each) white or pinto beans, rinsed and drained
1 can (15 ounces) red kidney beans, rinsed and drained
1 cup beef broth
1 medium onion, chopped
2 cloves garlic, minced
1 teaspoon salt
1 teaspoon grated lemon peel
1 teaspoon dried thyme leaves
1 teaspoon black pepper
Chopped fresh parsley

1. Place beef, beans, broth, onion, garlic, salt, lemon peel, thyme and pepper into slow cooker. Cover; cook on LOW 8 to 9 hours.

2. Adjust seasonings before serving, if desired. Arrange beef on top of beans. Garnish with parsley.   *Makes 6 to 8 servings*

Slow Cooker Stew

1 pound beef for stew
1 package (1 ounce) au jus mix
2 cans (15 ounces each) beef broth
1 pound potatoes, peeled and diced
½ pound carrots, peeled and cut into 2-inch pieces *or* ½ pound baby carrots
2 medium onions, chopped
   Water
1 bag (16 ounces) frozen peas, thawed
1 tablespoon cornstarch

1. Place stew meat in slow cooker. Add au jus mix, broth, potatoes, carrots, onions and enough water to cover. Cover; cook on LOW 8 hours.

2. Add peas one hour before serving, .

3. Just before serving, sprinkle with cornstarch and stir. Cook 5 minutes to thicken sauce.

Makes 4 to 6 servings

Variation: Substitute a cut-up chicken for the stew meat and add chicken broth instead of beef broth. Omit the au jus mix for a delicious chicken stew.

Easy Beef Stroganoff

  3 cans (10¾ ounces each) condensed cream of chicken soup or cream of
      mushroom soup
  1 cup sour cream
  ½ cup water
  1 package (1 ounce) dry onion soup mix
  2 pounds beef for stew

Combine soup, sour cream, water and soup mix in slow cooker. Add beef; stir until well
coated. Cover; cook on HIGH 3 hours or on LOW 6 hours.   *Makes 4 to 6 servings*

Serving Suggestion: Serve over rice or noodles with a salad and hot bread.

Shredded Beef Fajitas

  1½ pounds beef flank steak
  1 cup chopped onion
  1 green bell pepper, cut into ½-inch pieces
  1 package (about 1½ ounces) fajita seasoning mix
  2 cloves garlic, minced *or* ¼ teaspoon garlic powder
  1 can (14½ ounces) diced tomatoes with jalapeños, undrained
  12 (8-inch) flour tortillas
      Toppings: sour cream, guacamole, shredded Cheddar cheese, salsa

1. Cut flank steak into 6 portions. Combine beef, onion, bell pepper, garlic and fajita seasoning
mix. Add tomatoes. Cover; cook on LOW 8 to 10 hours or on HIGH 4 to 5 hours.

2. Remove beef from slow cooker; shred. Return beef to slow cooker and stir. To serve fajitas,
place meat mixture evenly into flour tortillas. Add toppings as desired; roll up tortillas.
                                                          Makes 12 servings

Easy Beef Stroganoff

Italian Pot Roast

1 beef chuck shoulder roast (2 to 3 pounds)
1 can (28 ounces) crushed tomatoes, undrained *or* 6 to 8 fresh Roma tomatoes, chopped
1 package (about 1 ounce) dry spaghetti sauce seasoning mix
1 teaspoon minced garlic *or* ½ teaspoon garlic powder
1 teaspoon Italian seasoning blend
1 package (1 pound) spaghetti or other pasta, cooked
Grated Parmesan cheese

1. Place all ingredients except spaghetti and grated cheese in slow cooker. Cover; cook on HIGH 5 to 6 hours.

2. Serve sliced roast over spaghetti. Sprinkle with grated cheese.   *Makes 6 to 8 servings*

Serving Suggestion: Serve with salad and fresh Italian bread for a complete meal.

Roast Beef with Mushrooms and Vegetables

1 tablespoon vegetable oil
1 boneless beef chuck shoulder roast (3 to 5 pounds)
6 medium potatoes, peeled and halved
1 bag (1 pound) baby carrots
1 medium onion, quartered
1 can (10¾ ounces) condensed cream of mushroom soup
1 can (4 ounces) sliced mushrooms, drained
1 cup water

1. Heat oil in large skillet over medium-low heat. Brown roast on all sides. Drain excess fat. Place roast in slow cooker. Add potatoes, carrots and onion around roast.

2. Combine soup, mushrooms and water together in medium bowl. Pour over roast. Cover; cook on LOW 6 to 8 hours. *Makes 8 servings*

SLOW COOKING SECRET

For any roast larger than 2½ pounds, cut it in half so it cooks completely in the slow cooker.

Easy Family Burritos

1 beef roast (2 to 3 pounds)
1 jar (24 ounces) *or* **2 jars (16 ounces each) salsa**
Flour tortillas

1. Place roast in slow cooker; top with salsa. Cover; cook on LOW 8 to 10 hours.

2. Remove meat from slow cooker. Shred with 2 forks. Return to slow cooker; cook another 1 to 2 hours.

3. Serve shredded meat wrapped in tortillas.   *Makes 8 servings*

Serving Suggestion: Garnish your burritos with any combination of the following: shredded cheese, sour cream, salsa, lettuce, tomato, onion, guacamole, etc.

Helpful Hint: Freeze cooked burrito mixture in family-size portions. Reheat in the microwave over for a quick and easy dinner on busy nights when there is no time to cook.

Beef Boogie Woogie

   1 can (10¾ ounces) condensed cream of mushroom soup
   ½ cup chicken broth
   1 package (1 ounce) dry onion soup mix
   ½ teaspoon dried thyme leaves
   2 pounds lean beef for stew
   2 cups baby carrots
   8 ounces mushrooms, sliced

1. Combine mushroom soup, broth, soup mix and thyme in slow cooker; mix well.

2. Add remaining ingredients and stir until evenly coated. Cover; cook on HIGH 4 hours or on LOW 8 to 10 hours or until meat is tender. *Makes 8 servings*

Serving Suggestion: Serve over noodles or with mashed potatoes. Sprinkle with parsley.

Slow Cooker BBQ Beef

    1 beef chuck shoulder roast (3 pounds)
    1 cup water
    2 cubes beef bouillon
    1 can (15 ounces) tomato sauce
    ¼ cup brown sugar
    ¼ cup ketchup
    ¼ cup mustard
    1 tablespoon minced onion
      Dash Worcestershire sauce

1. Place roast, water and bouillon cubes in slow cooker. Cover; cook on LOW 8 to 10 hours or until tender.

2. Remove meat; shred with fork.

3. Discard all but 1 cup cooking liquid. Add remaining ingredients and shredded meat to slow cooker. Cover; cook on LOW 3 to 4 hours or on HIGH 1½ to 2 hours.   *Makes 6 to 8 servings*

Serving Suggestion: Serve on your favorite rolls for a great sandwich.

SLOW COOKING SECRET

Because slow cookers cook at a low heat for a long time, they are perfect for dishes calling for less-tender cuts of meat.

Main-Dish Pork

Cajun-Style Country Ribs

2 cups baby carrots
1 large onion, coarsely chopped
1 large green bell pepper, cut into 1-inch pieces
1 large red bell pepper, cut into 1-inch pieces
2 teaspoons minced garlic
2 tablespoons Cajun or Creole seasoning mix, divided
3½ to 4 pounds country-style pork spareribs
1 can (14½ ounces) stewed tomatoes, undrained
2 tablespoons water
1 tablespoon cornstarch
Hot cooked rice

1. Place carrots, onion, bell peppers, garlic and 2 teaspoons seasoning mix in slow cooker; mix well. Trim excess fat from ribs. Cut into individual riblets. Sprinkle 1 tablespoon seasoning mix over ribs; place in slow cooker over vegetables. Pour tomatoes with juice over ribs (slow cooker will be full). Cover; cook on LOW 6 to 8 hours or until ribs are fork tender.

2. Remove ribs and vegetables from cooking liquid to serving platter. Let liquid stand 5 minutes to allow fat to rise. Skim off fat.

3. Blend water, cornstarch and remaining 1 teaspoon Cajun seasoning. Stir into liquid in slow cooker. Cook on HIGH until sauce is thickened. Return ribs and vegetables to sauce; carefully stirring to coat. Serve with rice.   *Makes 6 servings*

Cajun-Style Country Ribs

Pork Meatballs & Sauerkraut

1¼ pounds lean ground pork
¾ cup dry bread crumbs
1 egg, slightly beaten
2 tablespoons milk
2 teaspoons caraway seeds, divided
1 teaspoon salt
½ teaspoon Worcestershire sauce
¼ teaspoon black pepper
1 bag (32 ounces) sauerkraut, drained, squeezed dry and snipped
½ cup chopped onion
6 slices bacon, crisp-cooked and crumbled
Chopped parsley

1. Combine ground pork, bread crumbs, egg, milk, 1 teaspoon caraway seeds, salt, Worcestershire and pepper in large bowl. Shape mixture into 2-inch balls. Brown meatballs in large nonstick skillet over medium-high heat.

2. Combine sauerkraut, onion, bacon and remaining 1 teaspoon caraway seeds in slow cooker. Place meatballs on top of sauerkraut mixture. Cover; cook on LOW 6 to 8 hours. Garnish with chopped parsley. *Makes 4 to 6 servings*

Pork Meatballs & Sauerkraut

Sweet & Saucy Ribs

2 pounds pork baby back ribs
1 teaspoon black pepper
2½ cups barbecue sauce (not mesquite flavored)
1 jar (8 ounces) cherry jam or preserves
1 tablespoon Dijon mustard
¼ teaspoon salt
Additional salt and black pepper (optional)

1. Trim excess fat from ribs. Rub 1 teaspoon black pepper over ribs. Cut ribs into 2-rib portions; place into slow cooker.

2. Combine barbecue sauce, jam, mustard and salt in small bowl; pour over ribs. Cover; cook on LOW 6 to 8 hours or until ribs are tender. Season with additional salt and pepper, if desired. Serve ribs with sauce. *Makes 4 servings*

Peking Pork Chops

6 pork chops, about 1 inch thick
½ cup soy or teriyaki sauce
¼ cup brown sugar
¼ cup Chinese ketchup or ketchup
1 teaspoon ground ginger
1 to 2 cloves garlic, crushed
Salt
Black pepper

1. Trim excess fat from pork chops. Place chops into slow cooker.

2. Combine soy sauce, brown sugar, ketchup, ginger and garlic in small bowl; pour over meat. Cover; cook on LOW 4 to 6 hours or until pork is tender. Season with salt and pepper, if desired. *Makes 6 servings*

Sweet & Saucy Ribs

Ham Meat Loaf with Horseradish Sauce

1½ pounds meat loaf mix* or ground beef
½ pound cooked ham, finely chopped
1 cup plain dry bread crumbs
1 cup finely chopped onion
2 large eggs, slightly beaten
½ cup chili sauce or ketchup
1 teaspoon plus ⅛ teaspoon salt, divided
½ teaspoon caraway seeds
¼ teaspoon black pepper
½ cup sour cream
3 tablespoons thinly sliced green onions
1 tablespoon prepared horseradish
1 tablespoon spicy brown or coarse-grained mustard

*Meat loaf mix is a combination of ground beef, pork and veal; see your meat retailer or make your own with 1 pound lean ground beef, ¼ pound ground pork and ¼ pound ground veal.

1. Combine meat loaf mix, ham, bread crumbs, onion, eggs, chili sauce, 1 teaspoon salt, caraway seeds and pepper in large bowl; mix well. Shape meat mixture into 7-inch round loaf.

2. Make foil handles using technique described below. Place meat loaf on top of foil strips. Using strips, place meat loaf into slow cooker. Cover; cook on LOW 4 to 4½ hours or until meat thermometer inserted into center of meat loaf reads 165°F. Use foil strips to remove meat loaf from slow cooker. Let stand 5 minutes.

3. Meanwhile, combine sour cream, green onions, horseradish, mustard and remaining ⅛ teaspoon salt in small bowl; mix well. Cut meat loaf into wedges; serve with horseradish sauce. *Makes 8 servings*

Foil Handles: Tear off three 18 x 2-inch strips of heavy foil or use regular foil folded to double thickness. Crisscross foil strips in spoke design as shown on page 7.

Autumn Harvest Sausage and Cabbage

1 package (12 ounces) reduced-fat pork sausage
8 cups chopped red cabbage (1 small head)
3 potatoes, diced
3 apples, diced
1 onion, sliced
½ cup sugar
½ cup white vinegar
1 teaspoon salt
½ teaspoon black pepper
½ teaspoon ground allspice
¼ teaspoon ground cloves

1. Cook sausage in large nonstick skillet over medium-high heat until no longer pink, stirring to separate; drain fat.

2. Combine sausage and remaining ingredients in large bowl; mix well. Spoon mixture into slow cooker. Cover; cook on LOW 8 to 10 hours or until potatoes are tender.

Makes 6 to 8 servings

Note: It is easier to mix all the ingredients in a large bowl instead of the slow cooker because the slow cooker will be filled to the top until the cabbage cooks down.

Shredded Pork Wraps

1 cup salsa, divided
2 tablespoons cornstarch
1 bone-in pork sirloin roast (2 pounds)
6 (8-inch) flour tortillas
3 cups broccoli slaw mix
⅓ cup shredded reduced-fat Cheddar cheese

1. Combine ¼ cup salsa and cornstarch in small bowl; stir until smooth. Pour mixture into slow cooker. Top with pork roast. Pour remaining ¾ cup salsa over roast.

2. Cover; cook on LOW 6 to 8 hours or until internal temperature reaches 165°F when tested with meat thermometer inserted in thickest part of roast, not touching bone. Transfer roast to cutting board; cover with foil and let stand 10 to 15 minutes or until cool enough to handle. (Internal temperature will rise 5° to 10°F during stand time.) Trim and discard outer fat from pork. Using 2 forks, pull pork into coarse shreds.

3. Divide shredded meat evenly among tortillas. Spoon about 2 tablespoons salsa mixture on top of meat in each tortilla. Top evenly with broccoli slaw and cheese. Fold bottom edge of tortilla over filling; fold in sides. Roll up completely to enclose filling. Serve remaining salsa mixture as dipping sauce.

Makes 6 servings

Shredded Pork Wrap

Cantonese Pork

1 tablespoon vegetable oil
2 pounds pork tenderloin, cut into strips
1 can (8 ounces) pineapple tidbits
1 can (8 ounces) tomato sauce
2 cans (4 ounces each) sliced mushrooms, drained
1 medium onion, thinly sliced
3 tablespoons brown sugar
2 tablespoons Worcestershire sauce
1½ teaspoons salt
1½ teaspoons white vinegar
Hot cooked rice

1. Heat oil in large nonstick skillet over medium-low heat. Brown pork on all sides. Drain excess fat.

2. Place all ingredients into slow cooker. Cover; cook on HIGH 4 hours or on LOW 6 to 8 hours.

3. Serve over rice.

Makes 8 servings

SLOW COOKING SECRET

Most manufacturers recommend that slow cookers be one-half to three-quarters full for the best results.

Cantonese Pork

Cajun Sausage and Rice

8 ounces kielbasa sausage, cut in ¼-inch slices
1 can (14½ ounces) diced tomatoes, undrained
1 medium onion, diced
1 medium green bell pepper, diced
2 ribs celery, thinly sliced
1 tablespoon chicken bouillon granules
1 tablespoon steak sauce
3 bay leaves *or* **1 teaspoon dried thyme leaves**
1 teaspoon sugar
¼ to ½ teaspoon hot pepper sauce
1 cup uncooked instant rice
½ cup water
½ cup chopped parsley (optional)

1. Combine sausage, tomatoes with juice, onion, bell pepper, celery, bouillon, steak sauce, bay leaves, sugar and hot pepper sauce in slow cooker. Cover; cook on LOW 8 hours or on HIGH 4 hours.

2. Remove bay leaves; stir in rice and water. Cook on HIGH 25 minutes or until rice is done. Stir in parsley, if desired.   *Makes 5 servings*

Hearty White Beans and Ham

1 package (16 ounces) dried navy beans or mixed dried beans
   Water
1 meaty ham bone
1 can (14½ ounces) tomatoes with green chilies, undrained
1 medium potato, diced
1 stalk celery, diced
½ small onion, diced
½ envelope dried onion soup mix
1 tablespoon Worcestershire sauce
1 teaspoon salt
½ teaspoon black pepper

1. Sort, rinse and drain beans. Place in Dutch oven; cover with water. Bring to a boil; reduce heat and simmer 1 hour. Drain water from beans; return to soup pot. Add ham bone and enough water to cover generously. Cook 1 to 2 hours over low heat. Remove ham bone; pull meat from bone.

2. Transfer beans, liquid, ham bone and meat to slow cooker. Add remaining ingredients; mix well. Cover; cook on LOW 6 to 8 hours or until beans are done. Remove and discard ham bone.
Makes 10 servings

Barbecued Pulled Pork

    3 to 4 pound boneless pork shoulder or butt roast
    1 teaspoon salt
    1 teaspoon ground cumin
    1 teaspoon paprika
    1 teaspoon black pepper
    ½ teaspoon ground red pepper
    1 medium onion, thinly sliced
    1 medium green bell pepper, cut into strips
    1 bottle (18 ounces) barbecue sauce
    ½ cup packed light brown sugar
    Hot cooked rice
    Flour tortillas

1. Trim excess fat from pork. Combine salt, cumin, paprika, black pepper and red pepper in small bowl; rub over roast.

2. Place onion and bell pepper in slow cooker; add pork. Combine barbecue sauce and brown sugar; pour over meat. Cover; cook on LOW 8 to 10 hours.

3. Transfer roast to cutting board. Trim and discard fat from roast. Using 2 forks, pull pork into coarse shreds.

4. Serve pork and sauce over rice with tortillas.

Makes 4 to 6 servings

Barbecued Pulled Pork

Panama Pork Stew

    2 small sweet potatoes, peeled and cut into 2-inch pieces
       (about 12 ounces total)
    1 package (10 ounces) frozen corn
    1 package (9 ounces) frozen cut green beans
    1 cup chopped onion
 1¼ pounds lean pork stew meat, cut into 1-inch cubes
    1 can (14½ ounces) diced tomatoes, undrained
   ¼ cup water
    1 to 2 tablespoons chili powder
   ½ teaspoon salt
   ½ teaspoon ground coriander

1. Place potatoes, corn, green beans and onion in slow cooker. Top with pork.

2. Combine tomatoes with juice, water, chili powder, salt and coriander in large bowl. Pour over pork in slow cooker. Cover; cook on LOW 7 to 9 hours. *Makes 6 servings*

SLOW COOKING SECRET

To remove a small amount of fat from dishes cooked in the slow cooker, lightly pull a sheet of clean paper towel over the surface, letting the grease be absorbed by the paper towel. Repeat this process if necessary.

Panama Pork Stew

Ham and Potato Casserole

    1½ pounds red potatoes, peeled and sliced
    8 ounces thinly sliced ham
    2 poblano chili peppers, cut into thin strips
    2 tablespoons olive oil
    1 tablespoon dried oregano leaves
    ¼ teaspoon salt
    1 cup (4 ounces) shredded Monterey Jack cheese with or without hot peppers
    2 tablespoons finely chopped fresh cilantro

1. Combine all ingredients except cheese and cilantro in slow cooker; mix well. Cover; cook on LOW 7 hours or on HIGH 4 hours.

2. Transfer potato mixture to serving dish; sprinkle with cheese and cilantro. Let stand 3 minutes or until cheese melts. *Makes 6 to 7 servings*

Lemon Pork Chops

    1 tablespoon vegetable oil
    4 boneless pork chops
    3 cans (8 ounces each) tomato sauce
    1 large onion, quartered and sliced
    1 large green bell pepper, cut into strips
    1 tablespoon lemon-pepper seasoning
    1 tablespoon Worcestershire sauce
    1 large lemon, quartered

1. Heat oil in large skillet over medium-low heat. Brown pork chops on both sides. Drain excess fat. Place pork in slow cooker.

2. Combine tomato sauce, onion, bell pepper, lemon-pepper seasoning and Worcestershire sauce in slow cooker. Squeeze juice from lemon quarters over mixture; drop squeezed peels into slow cooker. Cover; cook on LOW 6 to 8 hours or until pork is tender. Remove and discard lemon peels. *Makes 4 servings*

Peachy Pork

2 cans (about 15 ounces each) sliced peaches in heavy syrup, undrained
6 to 8 boneless pork blade or top loin chops (about 2 pounds)
1 small onion, thinly sliced
½ cup golden raisins
¼ cup packed light brown sugar
3 tablespoons cider vinegar
2 tablespoons tapioca
1 teaspoon salt
¾ teaspoon cinnamon
¼ teaspoon red pepper flakes
2 tablespoons cornstarch
2 tablespoons water

1. Cut peach slices in half with spoon. Place peaches with juice, pork chops, onion, raisins, sugar, vinegar, tapioca, salt, cinnamon and pepper flakes into slow cooker. Cover; cook on LOW 7 to 8 hours.

2. Remove pork to warm platter. Skim off fat from peach mixture. Combine cornstarch and water to make smooth paste. Stir into peach mixture. Cook on HIGH 15 minutes or until sauce is thickened. Adjust seasonings, if desired.

Makes 7 to 8 hours

Red Beans and Rice with Ham

    1 package (1 pound) dried red beans
    1 pound beef smoked sausage, sliced
    1 ham slice, cubed (about 8 ounces)
    1 small onion, diced
2½ to 3 cups water
    1 teaspoon adobo seasoning with pepper
⅛ teaspoon ground red pepper
    Hot cooked rice

1. Soak beans overnight; rinse and drain.

2. Place beans in slow cooker. Add sausage, ham, onion and water (3 cups for HIGH; 2½ cups for LOW). Season with adobo seasoning and pepper.

3. Cover; cook on HIGH 3 to 4 hours or on LOW 7 to 8 hours or until beans are done, stirring every 2 hours, if necessary.

4. Serve over rice.

Makes 6 servings

SLOW COOKING SECRET

Recipes often provide a range of cooking times in order to account for variables such as the temperature of the ingredients before cooking, the quantity of food in the slow cooker and the altitude.

Red Beans and Rice with Ham

Italian-Style Sausage with Rice

     1 pound mild Italian sausage, cut in 1-inch pieces
     1 can (29 ounces) pinto beans, rinsed and drained
     1 cup spaghetti sauce
     1 green bell pepper, cut into strips
     1 small onion, halved and sliced
     ½ teaspoon salt
     ¼ teaspoon black pepper
        Hot cooked rice
        Chopped fresh basil

1. Brown sausage in large nonstick skillet over medium heat. Pour off drippings. Place sausage, beans, spaghetti sauce, bell pepper, onion, salt and pepper into slow cooker. Cover; cook on LOW 4 to 6 hours.

2. Serve with rice. Garnish with basil, if desired.   *Makes 4 to 5 servings*

Ham & Potato Scallop

     8 slices ham
     4 medium potatoes, thinly sliced
     1 large onion, sliced
        Salt
        Black pepper
     1 cup corn
     1 can (10¾ ounces) condensed cream of mushroom soup
     1 cup (4 ounces) shredded Cheddar cheese
     1 tablespoon Worcestershire sauce

1. Layer ham, potatoes and onion in slow cooker; season with salt and pepper. Add corn.

2. Combine soup, cheese and Worcestershire sauce in medium bowl. Pour over ham mixture. Cover; cook on LOW 8 hours or until potatoes are done.   *Makes 8 servings*

Italian-Style Sausage with Rice

Two White Meats Together
(Marinated Pork and Chicken)

6 pounds boneless chicken pieces
2 pounds lean boneless pork, cubed
6 cups beef broth
2 cups sherry or apple juice
6 Roma tomatoes, chopped
2 teaspoons salt
4 cloves garlic, crushed
1 teaspoon dried rosemary leaves
1 teaspoon black pepper

1. Place chicken and pork in large bowl. To make marinade, combine remaining ingredients in large bowl. Pour half of marinade mixture over chicken and pork. Cover bowl; marinate meat in refrigerator 4 hours or overnight. Cover remaining marinade; refrigerate.

2. Drain and discard marinade from meats. Place meats into slow cooker. Add remaining marinade. Cover; cook on LOW 6 to 8 hours or until meat is tender. Adjust seasonings, if desired.

Makes 12 servings

Golden Harvest Pork Stew

   1 pound boneless pork cutlets, cut into 1-inch pieces
   2 tablespoons all-purpose flour, divided
   1 tablespoon vegetable oil
   2 medium Yukon gold potatoes, unpeeled and cut into 1-inch cubes
   1 large sweet potato, peeled and cut into 1-inch cubes
   1 cup chopped carrots
   1 ear corn, broken into 4 pieces *or* ½ cup corn
½ cup chicken broth
   1 jalapeño pepper, seeded and finely chopped
   1 clove garlic, minced
   1 teaspoon salt
¼ teaspoon black pepper
¼ teaspoon dried thyme leaves

1. Toss pork pieces with 1 tablespoon flour; set aside. Heat oil in large nonstick skillet over medium-high heat until hot. Brown pork 2 to 3 minutes per side; transfer to 5-quart slow cooker.

2. Add remaining ingredients to slow cooker. Cover; cook on LOW 5 to 6 hours.

3. Combine remaining 1 tablespoon flour and ¼ cup broth from stew in small bowl; stir until smooth. Stir flour mixture into stew. Cook on HIGH 10 minutes or until thickened. Adjust seasonings, if desired.

Makes 4 to 5 servings

SLOW COOKING SECRET
Trim excess fat from meat before putting in the slow cooker to help reduce the fat.

Honey Ribs

    1 can (10¾ ounces) condensed beef consommé
    ½ cup water
    3 tablespoons soy sauce
    2 tablespoons honey
    2 tablespoons maple syrup
    2 tablespoons barbecue sauce
    ½ teaspoon dry mustard
    2 pounds extra-lean baby back ribs

1. Combine all ingredients except ribs in slow cooker; mix well.

2. Add ribs to slow cooker. (If ribs are especially fatty, broil 10 minutes before adding to slow cooker.) Cover; cook on LOW 6 to 8 hours or on HIGH to 4 hours or until ribs are tender.

Makes 4 servings

Simple Slow Cooker Pork Roast

    4 to 5 red potatoes, cut into bite-size pieces
    4 carrots, cut into bite-size pieces
    1 marinated pork roast (any size)
    ½ cup water
    1 package (10 ounces) frozen baby peas, thawed

1. Place potatoes, carrots and pork roast into slow cooker. Add water. Cover; cook on LOW 6 to 8 hours or until vegetables are done.

2. Add peas during last hour of cooking. Adjust seasonings, if desired.

Makes 6 servings

Honey Ribs

Pork and Mushroom Ragout

        1 boneless pork loin roast (1¼ pounds)
    1¼ cups canned crushed tomatoes, divided
        2 tablespoons cornstarch
        2 teaspoons dried savory leaves
        3 sun-dried tomatoes, chopped
        1 package (8 ounces) sliced mushrooms
        1 large onion, sliced
        1 teaspoon black pepper
        3 cups hot cooked noodles

1. Spray large nonstick skillet with nonstick cooking spray; heat skillet over medium heat until hot. Brown roast on all sides; set aside.

2. Place ½ cup crushed tomatoes, cornstarch, savory and sun-dried tomatoes into slow cooker; mix well. Layer mushrooms, onion and roast over tomato mixture.

3. Pour remaining tomatoes over roast; sprinkle with pepper. Cover; cook on LOW 4 to 6 hours or until internal temperature reaches 165°F when tested with meat thermometer inserted into the thickest part of roast.

4. Transfer roast to cutting board; cover with foil. Let stand 10 to 15 minutes. Internal temperature will continue to rise 5° to 10°F during stand time.

5. Slice roast. Serve with sauce over hot cooked noodles.   *Makes 6 servings*

Pork and Mushroom Ragout

Orange Teriyaki Pork

   1 pound lean pork stew meat, cut into 1-inch cubes
   1 package (16 ounces) frozen pepper blend for stir-fry
   4 ounces sliced water chestnuts
  ½ cup orange juice
   2 tablespoons quick-cooking tapioca
   2 tablespoons packed light brown sugar
   2 tablespoons teriyaki sauce
  ½ teaspoon ground ginger
  ½ teaspoon dry mustard
1⅓ cups hot cooked rice

1. Spray large nonstick skillet with nonstick cooking spray; heat skillet over medium heat until hot. Add pork; brown on all sides. Remove from heat; set aside.

2. Place peppers and water chestnuts in slow cooker. Top with browned pork. Mix orange juice, tapioca, brown sugar, teriyaki sauce, ginger and mustard in large bowl. Pour over pork mixture in slow cooker. Cover; cook on LOW 3 to 4 hours.

3. Serve with rice.

Makes 4 servings

SLOW COOKING SECRET

Slow cooking may take longer in high altitudes. Allow an additional 30 minutes for each hour of cooking time specified in the recipe.

Sauerkraut Pork Ribs

1 tablespoon vegetable oil
3 to 4 pounds country-style pork ribs
1 large onion, thinly sliced
1 teaspoon caraway seeds
½ teaspoon garlic powder
¼ to ½ teaspoon black pepper
¾ cup water
1 jar (about 28 ounces) sauerkraut
6 medium potatoes, quartered

1. Heat oil in large skillet over medium-low heat. Brown ribs on all sides; transfer ribs to slow cooker. Drain excess fat.

2. Add onion to skillet; cook until tender. Add caraway seeds, garlic powder and pepper; cook 15 minutes. Transfer onion mixture to slow cooker. Add water to skillet and scrape bottom of pan. Pour pan juices into slow cooker.

3. Partially drain sauerkraut, leaving some liquid; pour over meat in slow cooker. Top with potatoes. Cover; cook on LOW 6 to 8 hours or until potatoes are tender, mixing once during cooking. *Makes 12 servings*

Pork & Tomato Ragout

    2 pounds pork stew meat, cut into 1-inch pieces
¼ cup all-purpose flour
    3 tablespoons oil
1¼ cups white wine
    2 pounds red potatoes, cut into ½-inch pieces
    1 can (14½ ounces) diced tomatoes, undrained
    1 cup finely chopped onion
    1 cup water
½ cup finely chopped celery
    2 cloves garlic, minced
½ teaspoon black pepper
    1 cinnamon stick
    3 tablespoons chopped fresh parsley

1. Toss pork with flour. Heat oil in large skillet over medium-high heat. Add pork to skillet and brown on all sides. Place pork into slow cooker.

2. Add wine to skillet; bring to a boil, scraping up browned bits from bottom of skillet. Pour into slow cooker.

3. Add all remaining ingredients except parsley. Cover; cook on LOW 6 to 8 hours or until pork and potatoes are tender. Remove and discard cinnamon stick. Adjust seasonings, if desired. Sprinkle with parsley just before serving. *Makes 6 servings*

Pork & Tomato Ragout

Mediterranean Meatball Ratatouille

2 tablespoons olive oil, divided
1 pound bulk mild Italian sausage
1 package (8 ounces) sliced mushrooms
1 small eggplant, diced
1 zucchini, diced
½ cup chopped onion
1 clove garlic, minced
1 teaspoon dried oregano leaves, divided
1 teaspoon salt, divided
½ teaspoon black pepper, divided
2 tomatoes, diced
1 tablespoon tomato paste
2 tablespoons chopped fresh basil
1 teaspoon fresh lemon juice

1. Pour 1 tablespoon olive oil into 5-quart slow cooker. Shape sausage into 1-inch meatballs. Place half the meatballs in slow cooker. Add half the mushrooms, eggplant, zucchini. Top with onion, garlic, ½ teaspoon oregano, ½ teaspoon salt and ¼ teaspoon pepper.

2. Add remaining meatballs, mushrooms, eggplant and zucchini, ½ teaspoon oregano, ½ teaspoon salt and ¼ teaspoon pepper. Top with remaining 1 tablespoon olive oil. Cover; cook on LOW 6 to 7 hours.

3. Stir in diced tomatoes and tomato paste. Cover; cook on LOW 15 minutes. Stir in basil and lemon; serve.

Makes 6 (1⅔ cups) servings

Mediterranean Meatball Ratatouille

Curried Pork Pot

1 can (10¾ ounces) condensed cream of chicken soup
1 cup evaporated skimmed milk or water
1 medium onion, chopped
½ cup raisins
1 tablespoon mild curry powder
1 tablespoon dried parsley
1 teaspoon minced garlic
1 pound boneless country-style pork ribs
  Salt
  Black pepper
  Hot cooked rice, pasta or egg noodles

1. Combine soup, milk, onion, raisins, curry, parsley and garlic in large bowl; mix well. Add pork, stirring to coat.

2. Pour mixture into slow cooker. Cover; cook on LOW 6 to 8 hours or on HIGH 4 to 6 hours. Stir in salt and pepper to taste.

3. Serve over rice, pasta or noodles. *Makes 6 servings*

SLOW COOKING SECRET

Always taste the finished dish before serving. Adjust the seasoning to your preference by adding a small amount of salt, pepper, herbs and spices from the original recipe.

Easy Pork Chop Dinner

1 large onion, thinly sliced
3 to 4 medium baking potatoes, sliced
6 pork chops
1 can (10¾ ounces) reduced-fat condensed cream of celery soup
½ cup water or milk

1. Place onion then potatoes into slow cooker. Top with pork.

2. Combine soup and water in small bowl; pour over chops. Cover; cook on LOW 6 to 8 hours.

Makes 6 servings

Chili Verde

1 tablespoon vegetable oil
1 to 2 pounds boneless pork chops
Sliced carrots (enough to cover bottom of slow cooker)
1 jar (24 ounces) mild green chili salsa
Chopped onion (optional)

1. Heat oil in large skillet over medium-low heat. Brown pork on all sides. Drain excess fat.

2. Place carrot slices in bottom of slow cooker. Place pork on top of carrots. Pour salsa over chops. Add onion to taste, if desired. Cover; cook on HIGH 6 to 8 hours. Shred the pork and serve with tortillas, if desired.

Makes 4 to 8 servings

Simply Delicious Pork

  1½ **pounds boneless pork loin, sliced**
    4 **medium Yellow Delicious apples, sliced**
    3 **tablespoons brown sugar**
    1 **teaspoon cinnamon**
  ½ **teaspoon salt**

Place pork slices in bottom of slow cooker. Cover with apples. Combine brown sugar, cinnamon and salt in small bowl; sprinkle over apples. Cover; cook on LOW 6 to 8 hours.

Makes 6 servings

Slow-Cooked Pork Chops

    1 **teaspoon vegetable oil**
    6 **pork chops**
    1 **can (10¾ ounces) condensed cream of mushroom soup**
    1 **can (10¾ ounces) condensed cream of celery soup**
    1 **tablespoon beef bouillon granules**
      Salt
      Black pepper

1. Heat oil in large skillet over medium-low heat. Brown pork on both sides. Drain excess fat. Place pork into slow cooker.

2. Combine all ingredients in medium bowl; pour over pork. Cover; cook on LOW 6 hours or until pork is tender. Adjust seasonings, if desired. Serve over rice or mashed potatoes.

Makes 6 servings

Simply Delicious Pork

Sweet and Sour Spare Ribs

    4 pounds pork spare ribs
    2 cups dry sherry or chicken broth
    ½ cup pineapple, mango or guava juice
    ⅓ cup chicken broth
    2 tablespoons packed light brown sugar
    2 tablespoons cider vinegar
    2 tablespoons soy sauce
    1 clove garlic, minced
    ½ teaspoon salt
    ¼ teaspoon black pepper
    ⅛ teaspoon red pepper flakes
    2 tablespoons cornstarch

1. Preheat oven to 400°F. Place ribs in foil-lined shallow roasting pan. Bake 30 minutes, turning over after 15 minutes. Remove from oven. Slice meat into 2-rib portions. Place ribs in 5-quart slow cooker. Add remaining ingredients except cornstarch to slow cooker.

2. Cover; cook on LOW 6 hours. Transfer ribs to platter; keep warm. Let liquid in slow cooker stand 5 minutes to allow fat to rise. Skim off fat.

3. Combine cornstarch and ¼ cup liquid from slow cooker; stir until smooth. Stir mixture into liquid in slow cooker; mix well. Cook on HIGH 10 minutes or until slightly thickened.

Makes 4 servings

Sweet and Sour Spare Ribs

Succulent Pork Chops

        2 teaspoons olive oil
        6 boneless pork chops, ½ inch thick
        1 can (10¾ ounces) condensed cream of chicken soup
        1 can (10¾ ounces) condensed cream of mushroom soup
        1 can (8 ounces) sliced mushrooms, drained
        1 cup milk
        2 teaspoons minced garlic
          Salt
          Black pepper

1. Heat oil in large skillet over medium-low heat. Brown pork chops on both sides. Drain excess fat.

2. Place pork chops in slow cooker. Add remaining ingredients over top. Cover; cook on LOW 8 to 10 hours or on HIGH 5 to 7 hours. Adjust seasonings, if desired.

Makes 6 servings

SLOW COOKING SECRET

Do not use the slow cooker to reheat left-over foods. Transfer any cooled leftover food to a resealable plastic food-storage bag or plastic storage container with a tight-fitting lid and refrigerate. Use a microwave oven, the range top or oven for reheating.

Buck County Ribs

4 boneless country-style pork ribs
1 teaspoon salt
1 jar (about 28 ounces) sauerkraut, drained
1 medium apple, diced
1 tablespoon sugar
1 teaspoon chicken bouillon granules *or* 1 cup chicken broth
Mashed potatoes (optional)

1. Place ribs into slow cooker. Sprinkle with salt. Spoon sauerkraut over ribs. Top with apple; sprinkle sugar over apple. Add bouillon granules. Cover; cook on LOW 8 to 9 hours.

2. Serve with mashed potatoes, if desired.

Makes 4 servings

Fall Apart Pork Chops

2 teaspoons vegetable oil
4 center cut bone-in pork chops
1 can (10¾ ounces) condensed cream of mushroom soup
¼ cup water
¼ cup cooking wine (such as sherry or marsala) or apple juice

1. Heat oil in large skillet over medium-low heat. Brown pork chops on both sides; season as desired. Drain excess fat. Transfer pork chops to slow cooker.

2. Whisk together soup, water and wine in large bowl. Pour mixture over top or pork. Cover; cook on HIGH 3 hours or until meat is tender. (Cook longer for very thick chops.)

Makes 4 servings

Make-Ahead Poultry

Mexicali Chicken

2 medium green bell peppers, cut into thin strips
1 large onion, quartered and thinly sliced
4 chicken thighs
4 chicken drumsticks
1 tablespoon chili powder
2 teaspoons dried oregano leaves
1 jar (16 ounces) chipotle salsa
½ cup ketchup
2 teaspoons ground cumin
½ teaspoon salt
Hot cooked noodles

1. Place bell peppers and onion in slow cooker; top with chicken. Sprinkle chili powder and oregano evenly over chicken. Add salsa. Cover; cook on LOW 7 to 8 hours or until chicken is tender.

2. Remove chicken pieces to serving bowl; keep warm. Stir ketchup, cumin and salt into liquid in slow cooker. Cook, uncovered, on HIGH 15 minutes or until hot.

3. Pour mixture over chicken. Serve with noodles. *Makes 4 servings*

Helpful Hint: For thicker sauce, blend 1 tablespoon cornstarch and 2 tablespoons water. Stir into cooking liquid with ketchup, cumin and salt.

Mexicali Chicken

Turkey with Pecan-Cherry Stuffing

1 fresh or frozen boneless turkey breast (about 3- to 4-pounds)
2 cups cooked rice
⅓ cup chopped pecans
⅓ cup dried cherries or cranberries
1 teaspoon poultry seasoning
¼ cup peach, apricot or plum preserves
1 teaspoon Worcestershire sauce

1. Thaw turkey breast, if frozen. Remove and discard skin. Cut slices three fourths of the way through turkey at 1-inch intervals.

2. Stir together rice, pecans, cherries and poultry seasoning in large bowl. Stuff rice between slices. If needed, skewer turkey lengthwise to hold together.

3. Place turkey in slow cooker. Cover; cook on LOW 5 to 6 hours or until turkey registers 170°F on meat thermometer inserted into thickest part of breast, not touching stuffing.

4. Stir together preserves and Worcestershire sauce. Spoon over turkey. Cover; let stand for 5 minutes. Remove and discard skewer, if used.

Makes 8 servings

Turkey with Pecan-Cherry Stuffing

Chicken with Italian Sausage

    10 ounces bulk mild or hot Italian sausage
     6 boneless skinless chicken thighs
     1 can (about 15 ounces) white beans, rinsed and drained
     1 can (about 15 ounces) red beans, rinsed and drained
     1 cup chicken broth
     1 medium onion, chopped
     1 teaspoon black pepper
    ½ teaspoon salt
      Chopped fresh parsley

1. Brown sausage in large skillet over medium-high heat, stirring to separate; drain fat. Spoon into slow cooker.

2. Trim fat from chicken. Place chicken, beans, broth, onion, pepper and salt in slow cooker. Cover; cook on LOW 5 to 6 hours.

3. Adjust seasonings, if desired. Slice each chicken thigh on the diagonal. Serve with sausage and beans. Garnish with parsley, if desired. *Makes 6 servings*

SLOW COOKING SECRET

To reduce the amount of fat in slow cooker meals, degrease canned broths.

Turkey with Chunky Cherry Relish

1 bag (16 ounces) frozen dark cherries, coarsely chopped
1 can (14 ounces) diced tomatoes with jalapeños, undrained
1 package (6 ounces) dried cherry-flavored cranberries or dried cherries,
    coarsely chopped
2 small onions, thinly sliced
1 small green bell pepper, chopped
½ cup packed brown sugar
2 tablespoons tapioca
1½ tablespoons salt
½ teaspoon ground cinnamon
½ teaspoon black pepper
½ bone-in turkey breast (about 2½ to 3 pounds)
2 tablespoons water
1 tablespoon cornstarch

1. Place cherries, tomatoes with juice, cranberries, onions, bell pepper, brown sugar, tapioca, salt, cinnamon and black pepper in slow cooker; mix well.

2. Place turkey on top of mixture. Cover; cook on LOW 7 to 8 hours or until turkey registers 170°F on meat thermometer inserted into thickest part of breast, not touching bone.

3. Remove turkey from slow cooker; keep warm. Combine water and cornstarch to form smooth paste. Stir into cherry mixture. Cook, uncovered on HIGH 15 minutes or until thickened. Adjust seasoning, if desired. Slice turkey and top with relish.

Makes 4 to 6 servings

Slow-Simmered Curried Chicken

1½ cups chopped onions
1 medium green bell pepper, chopped
1 pound boneless skinless chicken breast or thighs, cut into bite-size pieces
1 cup medium salsa
2 teaspoons grated fresh ginger
½ teaspoon garlic powder
½ teaspoon red pepper flakes
¼ cup chopped fresh cilantro
1 teaspoon sugar
1 teaspoon curry powder
¾ teaspoon salt
   Hot cooked rice

1. Place onions and bell pepper in bottom of slow cooker. Top with chicken. Combine salsa, ginger, garlic powder and pepper flakes in small bowl; spoon over chicken. Cover; cook on LOW 5 to 6 hours or until chicken is tender.

2. Combine cilantro, sugar, curry powder and salt in small bowl. Stir mixture into slow cooker. Cover; cook on HIGH 15 minutes or until hot.

3. Serve with rice.

Makes 4 servings

Slow-Simmered Curried Chicken

Cheesy Slow Cooker Chicken

    6 boneless skinless chicken breasts
    Salt
    Black pepper
    Garlic powder
    2 cans (10¾ ounces each) condensed cream of chicken soup
    1 can (10¾ ounces) condensed Cheddar cheese soup
    Chopped fresh parsley (optional)

1. Place 3 chicken breasts in slow cooker. Sprinkle with salt, pepper and garlic powder. Repeat with remaining three breasts.

2. Mix soups together in medium bowl; pour over chicken. Cover; cook on LOW 6 to 8 hours. Garnish with parsley before serving, if desired.   *Makes 6 servings*

Orange Chicken

    1 pound boneless skinless chicken breasts
    1 can (12 ounces) orange soda
    ½ cup soy sauce
    Hot cooked rice

1. Place all ingredients except rice in slow cooker. Cover; cook on LOW 5 to 6 hours.

2. Serve over rice.   *Makes 4 servings*

Cheesy Slow Cooker Chicken

Tender Asian-Style Chicken

  6 to 8 boneless skinless chicken thighs
¼ cup flour
½ teaspoon black pepper
 1 tablespoon vegetable oil
¼ cup soy sauce
 2 tablespoons rice wine vinegar
 2 tablespoons ketchup
 1 tablespoon brown sugar
 1 clove garlic, minced
½ teaspoon grated fresh ginger or ¼ teaspoon ground ginger
¼ teaspoon red pepper flakes
    Hot cooked rice
    Chopped fresh cilantro (optional)

1. Trim visible fat from chicken. Combine flour and pepper in resealable plastic food storage bag. Add chicken; shake to coat with flour mixture.

2. Heat oil in large skillet over medium-high heat. Add chicken and brown about 2 minutes on each side. Place chicken in slow cooker.

3. Combine soy sauce, vinegar, ketchup, sugar, garlic, ginger and red pepper flakes in small bowl; pour over chicken. Cook on LOW 5 to 6 hours.

4. Serve with rice and garnish with cilantro, if desired.

Makes 4 to 6 servings

Sweet Jalapeño Mustard Turkey Thighs

3 turkey thighs, skin removed
¾ cup honey mustard
½ cup orange juice
1 tablespoon cider vinegar
1 teaspoon Worcestershire sauce
1 to 2 fresh jalapeño peppers,* finely chopped
1 clove garlic, minced
½ teaspoon grated orange peel

*Jalapeño peppers can sting and irritate the skin; wear rubber gloves when handling peppers and do not touch eyes. Wash hands after handling.

Place turkey thighs in single layer in slow cooker. Combine remaining ingredients in large bowl. Pour mixture over turkey thighs. Cover; cook on LOW 5 to 6 hours.

Makes 6 servings

SLOW COOKING SECRET

Skinless turkey is best for the slow cooker because the skin tends to shrivel and curl during cooking.

Greek-Style Chicken

6 boneless skinless chicken thighs
½ teaspoon salt
½ teaspoon black pepper
1 tablespoon olive oil
½ cup chicken broth
1 lemon, thinly sliced
¼ cup pitted kalamata olives
½ teaspoon dried oregano leaves
1 clove garlic, minced
   Hot cooked orzo or rice

1. Remove visible fat from chicken; sprinkle chicken with salt and pepper. Heat oil in large skillet over medium-high heat. Brown chicken on all sides. Place chicken in slow cooker.

2. Add broth, lemon, olives, oregano and garlic to slow cooker. Cover; cook on LOW 5 to 6 hours or until chicken is tender.

3. Serve with orzo.

Makes 4 to 6 servings

Greek-Style Chicken

Continental Chicken

        1 package (2¼ ounces) dried beef, cut up
        4 boneless skinless chicken breasts
        4 slices lean bacon
        1 can (10¾ ounces) condensed cream of mushroom soup
        ¼ cup all-purpose flour
        ¼ cup low-fat sour cream
           Hot cooked noodles

1. Spray slow cooker cooking surface with nonstick cooking spray. Place dried beef in bottom of slow cooker. Wrap each piece of chicken with one bacon strip. Place wrapped chicken on top of dried beef.

2. Combine soup, flour and sour cream in medium bowl until smooth. Pour over chicken. Cover; cook on LOW 7 to 9 hours or on HIGH 3 to 4 hours.

3. Serve over noodles.

Makes 4 servings

SLOW COOKING SECRET

One hour on HIGH equals 2 to 2½ hours on LOW for slow cookers that have the heat coils circling the crockery insert.

Continental Chicken

Southwestern-Style Chicken

6 to 8 boneless skinless chicken thighs or breasts
1 package (about 1¼ ounces) taco seasoning mix
¼ cup flour
2 tablespoons vegetable oil
1 large onion, cut into 1-inch pieces
2 green peppers, cut into 1-inch pieces
1 can (14½ ounces) diced tomatoes with jalapeños, undrained
Salt and pepper

1. Trim visible fat from chicken.

2. Reserve one teaspoon taco seasoning. Combine flour and remaining seasoning in plastic food storage bag. Add chicken, 1 to 2 pieces at a time; shake to coat.

3. Heat oil in large skillet over medium-high heat; brown chicken. Transfer chicken to slow cooker; sprinkle with reserved seasoning.

4. Add onion to skillet; cook and stir until translucent. Transfer onion to slow cooker. Top with green peppers and tomatoes with juice. Cover; cook on LOW 6 to 7 hours or until chicken is tender. Season with salt and pepper to taste.   *Makes 4 to 6 servings*

Black Bean and Turkey Stew

   3 cans (15 ounces each) black beans, drained and rinsed
1½ cups chopped onions
1½ cups fat-free reduced-sodium chicken broth
   1 cup sliced celery
   1 cup chopped red bell pepper
   4 cloves garlic, minced
1½ teaspoons dried oregano leaves
   ¾ teaspoon ground coriander
   ½ teaspoon ground cumin
   ¼ teaspoon ground red pepper
   6 ounces cooked turkey sausage, thinly sliced

1. Combine all ingredients in slow cooker, except sausage. Cover; cook on LOW 6 to 8 hours.

2. Transfer about 1½ cups bean mixture from slow cooker to blender or food processor; purée bean mixture. Return to slow cooker. Stir in sausage. Cover; cook on LOW an additional 10 to 15 minutes.   *Makes 6 servings*

SLOW COOKING SECRET
Sprinkle diced fresh tomatoes or snipped fresh herbs over slow cooker soups and stews to enhance color and flavor.

French Country Slow Cooker Chicken

1 medium onion, chopped
4 carrots, sliced
4 celery stalks, sliced
6 to 8 boneless skinless chicken breasts
1 teaspoon dried tarragon leaves
1 teaspoon dried thyme leaves
   Salt and black pepper, to taste
1 can (10¾ ounces) condensed cream of chicken soup
1 envelope (1 ounce) dried onion soup mix
⅓ cup white wine or apple juice
2 tablespoons cornstarch
   Hot cooked rice

1. Place onion, carrots and celery in bottom of slow cooker. Arrange chicken over vegetables. Sprinkle chicken with tarragon, thyme, salt and pepper. Pour soup over chicken. Sprinkle with onion soup mix. Cover; cook on HIGH 3 to 4 hours, stirring once.

2. Twenty minutes before serving, whisk together wine and cornstarch in small bowl. Stir until smooth. Pour mixture over chicken; stir well. Cook, uncovered, on HIGH 15 minutes or until sauce thickens.

3. Serve over rice.

Makes 6 servings

French Country Slow Cooker Chicken

Saucy Tropical Turkey

    1 small onion, halved and sliced
    3 to 4 turkey thighs, skin removed (about 2½ pounds)
    2 tablespoons cooking oil
    1 can (20 ounces) pineapple chunks, drained
    1 red bell pepper, cubed
    ⅔ cup apricot preserves
    3 tablespoons soy sauce
    1 teaspoon grated lemon peel
    1 teaspoon ground ginger
    ¼ cup cold water
    2 tablespoons cornstarch
    Hot cooked rice or noodles

1. Place onion in slow cooker.

2. Rinse turkey and pat dry. Heat oil in large skillet; brown turkey on all sides. Transfer to slow cooker and top with pineapple and bell pepper.

3. Combine preserves, soy sauce, lemon peel and ginger in small bowl; mix well. Spoon over turkey. Cover; cook on LOW 6 to 7 hours.

4. Remove turkey from slow cooker; keep warm. Blend water and cornstarch until smooth; stir into slow cooker. Cook on HIGH 15 minutes or until sauce is slightly thickened. Adjust seasonings, if desired. Return turkey to slow cooker; cook until hot.

5. Serve with rice.

Makes 6 servings

Country Captain Chicken

4 boneless skinless chicken thighs
2 tablespoons all-purpose flour
2 tablespoons vegetable oil, divided
1 cup chopped green bell pepper
1 large onion, chopped
1 rib celery, chopped
1 clove garlic, minced
¼ cup chicken broth
2 cups canned or fresh crushed tomatoes
½ cup golden raisins
1½ teaspoons curry powder
1 teaspoon salt
¼ teaspoon paprika
¼ teaspoon black pepper
2 cups hot cooked rice

1. Coat chicken with flour; set aside. Heat 1 tablespoon oil in large skillet over medium-high heat until hot. Add bell pepper, onion, celery and garlic. Cook and stir 5 minutes or until vegetables are tender. Place vegetables in slow cooker.

2. Heat remaining 1 tablespoon oil in same skillet over medium-high heat. Add chicken; cook 5 minutes per side. Place chicken in slow cooker.

3. Pour broth into skillet. Heat over medium-high heat, stirring frequently and scraping up any browned bits from bottom of skillet. Pour liquid into slow cooker. Add tomatoes, raisins, curry powder, salt, paprika and black pepper. Cover; cook on LOW 3 hours.

4. Serve chicken with sauce over rice.

Makes 4 servings

Gypsy's BBQ Chicken

6 boneless skinless chicken breasts
1 bottle (26 ounces) barbecue sauce
6 slices bacon
6 slices Swiss cheese

1. Place chicken in slow cooker. Cover with barbecue sauce. Cover; cook on LOW 8 to 9 hours.

2. Before serving, cut bacon strips in half. Cook bacon in microwave or on stovetop, keeping bacon flat.

3. Place 2 strips cooked bacon over each piece of chicken in slow cooker. Top with cheese slices. Cover; cook on HIGH until cheese melts.   *Makes 6 servings*

Note: If juices become too thick during cooking, add a little water.

SLOW COOKING SECRET

Do not cook whole chickens in the slow cooker because the temperature of the chicken cannot reach the desired level quickly enough for food safety.

Slow Cooker Chicken & Rice

3 cans (10¾ ounces each) condensed cream of chicken soup
2 cups quick-cooking rice
1 cup water
1 pound boneless skinless chicken breasts or breast tenders
½ teaspoon salt
¼ teaspoon black pepper
¼ teaspoon paprika
½ cup diced celery

Combine soup, rice and water in slow cooker. Add chicken; sprinkle with salt, pepper and paprika. Sprinkle celery over top of chicken. Cover; cook on HIGH 3 to 4 hours or on LOW 6 to 8 hours.

Makes 4 servings

SLOW COOKING SECRET

When adapting your own recipes for the slow cooker, use canned evaporated milk, nonfat dry milk or condensed soups instead of milk to make smooth sauces.

Slow Cooker Chicken & Rice

Chicken Parisienne

   6 boneless skinless chicken breasts, cubed
   ½ teaspoon salt
   ½ teaspoon black pepper
   ½ teaspoon paprika
   1 can (10¾ ounces) condensed cream of mushroom or cream of chicken soup
   2 cans (4 ounces each) sliced mushrooms, drained
   ½ cup dry white wine
   1 cup sour cream
   6 cups hot cooked egg noodles

1. Place chicken in slow cooker. Sprinkle with salt, pepper and paprika.

2. Add soup, mushrooms and wine to slow cooker; mix well. Cover; cook on HIGH 2 to 3 hours. In last 30 minutes of cooking, add sour cream.

3. Serve over noodles. Garnish as desired.

Makes 6 servings

SLOW COOKING SECRET

Dairy products should be added at the end of the cooking time, because they will curdle if cooked in the slow cooker for a long time.

Chicken Parisienne

Bonnie's Slow-Cooked Turkey Thighs with Potatoes

1 large onion, sliced
2 turkey thighs, skin removed
2 cloves garlic, minced
½ teaspoon black pepper
8 to 10 small red potatoes
1 can (12 ounces) beer *or* 1½ cups chicken broth
1 can (8 ounces) tomato sauce
1 bay leaf

Place onion slices on bottom of slow cooker. Place turkey thighs over onions; sprinkle with garlic and pepper. Place potatoes around turkey thighs. Add beer, tomato sauce and bay leaf. Cover; cook on LOW 8 to 10 hours. Remove and discard bay leaf. *Makes 2 to 4 servings*

Kat's Slow Chicken

1 cut-up whole chicken (3 pounds)
1 jar (26 ounces) spaghetti sauce
1 medium onion, sliced
1 medium green bell pepper, cut into strips
2 medium potatoes, cubed
1 carrot, sliced
1 rib celery, sliced
4 cloves garlic, minced
½ cup water

Combine all ingredients in slow cooker. Cover; cook on LOW 6 to 8 hours.

Makes 4 servings

Southwestern Turkey in Chilies and Cream

1 can (15 ounces) corn, drained
1 can (4 ounces) diced green chilies, drained
1 boneless skinless turkey breast, cut into 1-inch pieces
2 tablespoons plus 2 teaspoons flour, divided
1 tablespoon butter
½ cup chicken broth
1 clove garlic, minced
1 teaspoon salt
½ teaspoon paprika
¼ teaspoon dried oregano leaves
¼ teaspoon black pepper
½ cup heavy cream
2 tablespoons chopped fresh cilantro
3 cups hot cooked rice or pasta

1. Place corn and green chilies in slow cooker.

2. Coat turkey pieces with 2 tablespoons flour. Melt butter in large nonstick skillet over medium heat. Add turkey pieces; brown on all sides. Place turkey in slow cooker. Add broth, garlic, salt, paprika, oregano and pepper. Cover; cook on LOW 2 hours or until turkey is tender and no longer pink in center.

3. Combine cream and remaining 2 teaspoons flour in small bowl, stirring until smooth. Pour mixture into slow cooker. Cover; cook on HIGH 10 minutes or until slightly thickened. Stir in cilantro.

4. Serve over rice.

Makes 6 (1½-cup) servings

Mu Shu Turkey

    1 can (16 ounces) plums, drained, rinsed and pitted
    ½ cup orange juice
    ¼ cup finely chopped onion
    1 tablespoon minced fresh ginger
    ¼ teaspoon ground cinnamon
    1 pound boneless turkey breast, cut into thin strips
    6 (7-inch) flour tortillas
    3 cups coleslaw mix

1. Place plums in blender or food processor. Cover and blend until almost smooth. Combine plums, orange juice, onion, ginger and cinnamon in slow cooker; mix well. Place turkey over plum mixture. Cover; cook on LOW 3 to 4 hours.

2. Remove turkey from slow cooker and divide evenly among tortillas. Spoon about 2 tablespoons plum sauce over turkey in each tortilla; top with about ½ cup coleslaw mix. Fold bottom edge of tortilla over filling; fold in sides. Roll up to completely enclose filling. Repeat with remaining tortillas. Use remaining plum sauce for dipping.   *Makes 6 servings*

Mu Shu Turkey

Moroccan Chicken Tagine

        3 pounds chicken, cut into serving pieces and skin removed
        2 cups chicken broth
        1 can (14½ ounces) diced tomatoes, undrained
        2 onions, chopped
        1 cup dried apricots, chopped
        4 cloves garlic, minced
        2 teaspoons ground cumin
        1 teaspoon ground cinnamon
        1 teaspoon ground ginger
        ½ teaspoon ground coriander
        ½ teaspoon ground red pepper
        6 sprigs fresh cilantro
        1 tablespoon cornstarch
        1 tablespoon water
        1 can (15 ounces) chick-peas, drained and rinsed
        2 tablespoons chopped fresh cilantro
        ¼ cup slivered almonds, toasted
            Hot cooked couscous or rice

1. Place chicken in slow cooker. Combine broth, tomatoes with juice, onions, apricots, garlic, cumin, cinnamon, ginger, coriander, red pepper and cilantro sprigs in medium bowl; pour over chicken. Cover; cook on LOW 4 to 5 hours or until chicken is no longer pink in center. Transfer chicken to serving platter; cover to keep warm.

2. Combine cornstarch and water in small bowl; mix until smooth. Stir cornstarch mixture and chick-peas into slow cooker. Cover; cook on HIGH 15 minutes or until sauce is thickened. Pour sauce over chicken. Sprinkle with almonds and cilantro. Serve with couscous.

Makes 4 to 6 servings

Helpful Hint: To toast almonds, heat small nonstick skillet over medium-high heat. Add almonds; cook and stir about 3 minutes or until golden brown. Remove from pan at once. Let cool before adding to other ingredients.

Moroccan Chicken Tagine

Chicken and Chile Pepper Stew

1 pound boneless skinless chicken thighs, cut into ½-inch pieces
1 pound small potatoes, cut lengthwise in halves and then cut crosswise
    into slices
1 cup chopped onion
2 poblano chile peppers, seeded and cut into ½-inch pieces
1 jalapeño pepper,* seeded and finely chopped
3 cloves garlic, minced
3 cups fat-free reduced-sodium chicken broth
1 can (14½ ounces) no-salt-added diced tomatoes, undrained
2 tablespoons chili powder
1 teaspoon dried oregano leaves

Jalapeño peppers can sting and irritate the skin; wear rubber gloves when handling peppers and do not touch eyes. Wash hands after handling.

1. Place chicken, potatoes, onion, poblano peppers, jalapeño pepper and garlic into slow cooker.

2. Stir together broth, tomatoes with juice, chili powder and oregano in large bowl. Pour broth mixture over chicken mixture in slow cooker; mix well. Cover; cook on LOW 8 to 9 hours. *Makes 6 servings*

SLOW COOKING SECRET
Use freshly ground pepper for a quick simple flavor enhancer for slow cooker dishes.

My Favorite Chicken

1 cut-up whole chicken (about 3 pounds)
1 cup chopped onion
1 cup sliced celery
1 cup sliced carrots
½ teaspoon seasoning salt
½ teaspoon black pepper
¼ teaspoon garlic powder
¼ teaspoon poultry seasoning
3 to 4 medium potatoes, sliced
1 can (14 ounces) chicken broth

Place chicken pieces, onion, celery, carrots, seasoning salt, garlic powder, poultry seasoning and pepper into slow cooker. Top with potatoes. Pour broth over top. Cover; cook on HIGH 30 minutes. Turn to LOW; cook 6 to 8 hours. *Makes 4 servings*

Note: Use a slotted spoon and transfer solids to a bowl. Thicken the juice left in the slow cooker with a mixture of cornstarch and water.

Hot & Sour Chicken

4 to 6 boneless skinless chicken breasts
1 envelope (1 ounce) dried hot-and-sour soup mix
1 cup chicken or vegetable broth

Place chicken in slow cooker. Add soup mix and broth. Cover; cook on LOW 5 to 6 hours. Garnish as desired. *Makes 4 to 6 servings*

Serving Suggestions: Serve over steamed white rice and topped with crispy Chinese noodles. Or, for a colorful variation, serve it over a bed of snow peas and sugar snap peas tossed with diced red bell pepper.

Nice 'n' Easy Italian Chicken

1 pound boneless skinless chicken breasts
1 medium onion, chopped
8 ounces mushrooms, sliced
1 medium green bell pepper, chopped (optional)
1 medium zucchini, diced
1 jar (26 ounces) favorite spaghetti sauce

Combine all ingredients in slow cooker. Cover; cook on LOW 6 to 8 hours.

Makes 4 servings

Hot & Sour Chicken

Creamy Chicken and Mushrooms

    1 teaspoon salt
    ½ teaspoon black pepper
    ¼ teaspoon paprika
    3 boneless skinless chicken breasts, cut up
    1½ cups sliced fresh mushrooms
    ½ cup sliced green onions
    1¾ teaspoons chicken bouillon granules
    1 cup white wine
    ½ cup water
    1 can (5 ounces) evaporated milk
    5 teaspoons cornstarch
    Hot cooked rice

1. Combine salt, pepper and paprika in small bowl; sprinkle over chicken.

2. Layer chicken, mushrooms, green onions and bouillon in slow cooker. Pour wine and water over top. Cover; cook on HIGH 3 hours or on LOW 5 to 6 hours. Remove chicken and vegetables to platter; cover to keep warm.

3. Combine evaporated milk and cornstarch in small saucepan, stirring until smooth. Add 2 cups liquid from slow cooker; bring to a boil. Boil 1 minute or until thickened, stirring constantly.

4. Serve chicken over rice and top with sauce.

Makes 3 to 4 servings

Creamy Chicken and Mushrooms

Old World Chicken and Vegetables

  1 tablespoon dried oregano leaves
  1 teaspoon salt, divided
  1 teaspoon paprika
  ½ teaspoon garlic powder
  ¼ teaspoon black pepper
  2 medium green bell peppers, cut into thin strips
  1 small yellow onion, thinly sliced
  1 cut-up whole chicken (3 pounds)
  ⅓ cup ketchup
  6 ounces uncooked egg noodles

1. Combine oregano, ½ teaspoon salt, paprika, garlic powder and black pepper in small bowl; mix well.

2. Place bell peppers and onion in slow cooker. Top with chicken thighs and legs, sprinkle with half the oregano mixture, top with chicken breasts. Sprinkle chicken with remaining oregano mixture. Cover; cook on LOW 8 hours or on HIGH 4 hours. Stir in ketchup and remaining ½ teaspoon salt.

3. Just before serving, cook noodles following package directions; drain. Serve chicken and vegetables over noodles.

Makes 4 servings

Chicken Azteca

2 cups frozen corn
1 can (15 ounces) black beans, rinsed and drained
1 cup chunky salsa, divided
1 clove garlic, minced
½ teaspoon ground cumin
4 boneless skinless chicken breasts
1 package (8 ounces) cream cheese, cubed
Hot cooked rice
Shredded Cheddar cheese

1. Combine corn, beans, ½ cup salsa, garlic and cumin in slow cooker. Arrange chicken breasts over top; pour remaining ½ cup salsa over chicken. Cover; cook on HIGH 2 to 3 hours or on LOW 4 to 6 hours or until chicken is tender.

2. Remove chicken; cut into bite-size pieces. Return chicken to slow cooker; add cream cheese. Cook on HIGH until cream cheese melts and blends into sauce.

3. Spoon chicken and sauce over rice. Top with Cheddar cheese.   *Makes 4 servings*

SLOW COOKING SECRET
Skinless chicken is best for the slow cooker because the skin tends to shrivel and curl during cooking.

Heidi's Chicken Supreme

1 can (10¾ ounces) condensed cream of chicken soup
1 envelope (1 ounce) dried onion soup mix
6 boneless skinless chicken breasts
½ cup canned bacon crumbles *or* ½ pound bacon, crisp-cooked and crumbled
1 carton (16 ounces) reduced-fat sour cream

1. Spray slow cooker cooking surface with nonstick cooking spray. Combine soup with dried soup mix in medium bowl; mix well. Layer chicken breasts and soup mixture in slow cooker. Sprinkle with bacon crumbles.

2. Cover; cook on HIGH 4 hours or on LOW 8 hours. During last hour of cooking, stir in sour cream.
Makes 6 servings

Heather's Chicken Tetrazzini

4 to 6 boneless skinless chicken breasts
Garlic salt
Lemon-pepper seasoning
1 can (10¾ ounces) condensed cream of chicken soup
1 can (10¾ ounces) condensed cream of broccoli soup
1 package (16 ounces) spaghetti
Grated Parmesan cheese (optional)

1. Place chicken in slow cooker; sprinkle with garlic salt and lemon-pepper seasoning to taste. Pour soups over top. Cover; cook on LOW 6 to 8 hours.

2. Before serving, cook spaghetti according to package directions; drain. Serve chicken over spaghetti. Sprinkle with grated Parmesan cheese, if desired.
Makes 4 to 6 servings

Heidi's Chicken Supreme

Spicy Shredded Chicken

6 boneless skinless chicken breasts
1 jar of your favorite prepared salsa

Place chicken in slow cooker. Cover with salsa. Cover; cook on LOW 6 to 8 hours. Shred chicken with two forks before serving. *Makes 6 servings*

Serving Suggestion: Serve on warm flour tortillas with taco toppings

Creamy Chicken

3 boneless skinless chicken breasts *or* 6 boneless skinless thighs
2 cans (10¾ ounces each) condensed cream of chicken soup
1 can (14½ ounces) chicken broth
1 can (4 ounces) mushrooms, drained
½ medium onion, diced
 Salt to taste
 Black pepper to taste

Place all ingredients in slow cooker. Cover; cook on LOW 6 to 8 hours. *Makes 3 servings*

Variation: Add cubed American processed cheese food before serving.

Spicy Shredded Chicken

Chicken Cacciatore

¼ cup vegetable oil
2½ to 3 pounds chicken pieces
1 can (28 ounces) crushed Italian-style tomatoes
2 cans (8 ounces each) Italian-style tomato sauce
1 medium onion, chopped
1 can (4 ounces) sliced mushrooms, drained
2 cloves garlic, minced
1 teaspoon salt
1 teaspoon dried oregano leaves
½ teaspoon dried thyme leaves
½ teaspoon black pepper
Hot cooked spaghetti or rice

1. Heat oil in large skillet over medium-low heat. Brown chicken on all sides. Drain excess fat.

2. Transfer chicken to slow cooker. Add remaining ingredients except spaghetti. Cover; cook on LOW 6 to 8 hours.

3. Serve over spaghetti.

Makes 6 to 8 servings

Turkey Breast with Barley-Cranberry Stuffing

   2 cups fat-free reduced-sodium chicken broth
   1 cup quick-cooking barley
   ½ cup chopped onion
   ½ cup dried cranberries
   2 tablespoons slivered almonds, toasted
   ½ teaspoon rubbed sage
   ½ teaspoon garlic-pepper seasoning
   1 fresh or frozen bone-in turkey breast half (about 2 pounds), thawed and
      skinned
   ⅓ cup finely chopped fresh parsley

1. Combine broth, barley, onion, cranberries, almonds, sage and garlic-pepper seasoning in slow cooker.

2. Spray large nonstick skillet with nonstick cooking spray. Heat over medium heat until hot. Brown turkey breast on all sides; add to slow cooker. Cover; cook on LOW 3 to 4 hours or until internal temperature reaches 170°F when tested with meat thermometer inserted into the thickest part of breast, not touching bone.

3. Transfer turkey to cutting board; cover with foil and let stand 10 to 15 minutes before carving. Internal temperature will rise 5° to 10°F during stand time.

4. Stir parsley into sauce mixture in slow cooker. Serve sauce with sliced turkey.

Makes 6 servings

Herbed Turkey Breast with Orange Sauce

        1 large onion, chopped
        3 cloves garlic, minced
        1 teaspoon dried rosemary
        ½ teaspoon black pepper
        2 to 3 pounds boneless skinless turkey breast
    1½ cups orange juice
        2 tablespoons water
        1 tablespoon cornstarch

1. Place onion in slow cooker. Combine garlic, rosemary and pepper in small bowl; set aside. Cut slices about three fourths of the way through turkey at 2-inch intervals. Rub garlic mixture between slices.

2. Place turkey, cut side up, in slow cooker. Pour orange juice over turkey. Cover; cook on LOW 7 to 8 hours or until internal temperature reaches 170°F when tested with meat thermometer inserted into the thickest part of breast, not touching bone.

3. Transfer turkey to cutting board; cover with foil and let stand 10 to 15 minutes before carving. Internal temperature will rise 5° to 10°F during stand time.

4. Combine water and cornstarch, stirring until smooth. Stir into slow cooker juices. Cook on HIGH 15 minutes or until thickened. Serve sauce with sliced turkey.   *Makes 4 to 6 servings*

SLOW COOKING SECRET

Defrost meats and vegetables before cooking them in the slow cooker.

Herbed Turkey Breast with Orange Sauce

Sweet Chicken Curry

   1 pound boneless skinless chicken breasts, cut into 1-inch pieces
   1 large green or red bell pepper, cut into 1-inch pieces
   1 large onion, sliced
   1 large tomato, seeded and chopped
   ½ cup prepared mango chutney
   ¼ cup water
   2 tablespoons cornstarch
1½ teaspoons curry powder
1⅓ cups hot cooked rice

1. Place chicken, bell pepper and onion in slow cooker. Top with tomato.

2. Mix chutney, water, cornstarch and curry powder in small bowl. Pour chutney mixture over chicken mixture into slow cooker. Cover; cook on LOW 3½ to 4½ hours.

3. Serve over rice.   *Makes 4 servings*

SLOW COOKING SECRET

Slow cooker recipes with raw meats should cook a minimum of 3 hours on LOW and reach an internal temperature of 165°F or above.

Sweet Chicken Curry

Nicole's Favorite Slow Cooker Chicken Cacciatore

6 boneless skinless chicken breasts
Garlic powder
Onion powder
Seasoned salt
Italian seasoning
Black pepper
10 ounces mushrooms, sliced
1 can (15 ounces) Italian-style tomato sauce
¼ cup red wine or chicken broth
8 ounces bow-tie pasta, cooked

1. Spray slow cooker with cooking spray for easy cleanup. Place chicken in slow cooker. Sprinkle generously with seasonings to taste.

2. Add mushrooms. Pour tomato sauce and wine over top. Cover; cook on LOW 6 hours.

3. Serve with cooked pasta.

Makes 6 servings

Slow Cooker Chicken and Dressing

4 boneless skinless chicken breasts
Salt
Black pepper
4 slices Swiss cheese
1 can (14½ ounces) chicken broth
2 cans (10¾ ounces each) condensed cream of chicken or celery or mushroom soup
3 cups packaged stuffing mix
½ cup butter, melted

1. Place chicken in bottom of slow cooker. Season with salt and pepper to taste.

2. Top each breast with cheese slice. Add broth and soups. Sprinkle stuffing mix over top; pour melted butter over all. Cover; cook on LOW 6 to 8 hours or on HIGH 3 to 4 hours.

Makes 4 servings

SLOW COOKING SECRET

When cooking in the slow cooker, the lower temperatures lessen the chance of scorching and burning foods.

Chicken and Stuffing

½ cup flour
¾ teaspoon seasoned salt
¾ teaspoon black pepper
 4 to 6 boneless skinless chicken breasts
¼ cup butter
 2 cans (10¾ ounces each) condensed cream of mushroom soup
½ cup water
 1 package (12 ounces) seasoned stuffing mix

1. Combine flour, seasoned salt and pepper in large resealable food storage bag. Dredge chicken in flour mixture. Melt butter in large skillet over medium heat. Brown both sides of chicken. Transfer chicken to slow cooker.

2. Mix together soup and water in medium bowl; pour soup mixture over top of chicken.

3. Follow package directions for stuffing, decreasing liquid by half. Add to slow cooker over chicken. Cover; cook on HIGH 3 to 4 hours.   *Makes 4 to 6 servings*

Chicken and Stuffing

Chicken Teriyaki

    1 pound boneless skinless chicken tenders
    1 can (6 ounces) pineapple juice
   ¼ cup soy sauce
    1 tablespoon sugar
    1 tablespoon minced fresh ginger
    1 tablespoon minced garlic
    1 tablespoon vegetable oil
    1 tablespoon molasses
  24 cherry tomatoes (optional)
    2 cups hot cooked rice

1. Combine all ingredients except rice in slow cooker. Cover; cook on LOW 2 hours or until chicken is tender.

2. Serve chicken and sauce over rice.

Makes 4 servings

SLOW COOKING SECRET

When adapting your favorite recipe to a slow cooker, you will want to reduce the liquid by as much as half, because slow-cooker cooking doesn't lose as much moisture as conventional cooking.

Turkey Spaghetti Sauce

1 tablespoon vegetable oil
2 pounds ground turkey
1 can (12 ounces) beer
1 jar (26 ounces) spaghetti sauce
1 can (6 ounces) tomato paste
1 envelope (1½ ounces) dried spaghetti sauce seasoning mix
  Water

1. Heat oil in large skillet over medium-low heat. Brown turkey, stirring to separate. Add beer; continue cooking until turkey is no longer pink.

2. Place turkey mixture in slow cooker. Add spaghetti sauce. Fill emptied sauce jar with water to rinse out remaining sauce. Pour jar full of water into slow cooker. Add tomato paste and dried spaghetti sauce seasoning mix. Cover; cook on LOW 6 to 8 hours. *Makes 8 servings*

SLOW COOKING SECRET

Avoid putting a hot slow cooker insert directly on a very cold surface. The insert could crack from the shock of the two extreme temperatures.

Coconut Chicken Curry

          1 tablespoon vegetable oil
          4 boneless skinless chicken breasts
          3 medium potatoes, peeled and chopped
          1 medium onion, sliced
          1 can (14 ounces) coconut milk
          1 cup chicken broth
     1½ teaspoons curry powder
          1 teaspoon hot pepper sauce (optional)
     ½ teaspoon salt
     ½ teaspoon black pepper
          1 package (10 ounces) frozen peas
          Hot cooked rice (optional)

1. Heat oil in medium skillet over medium-high heat. Brown chicken breasts on both sides. Place potatoes and onion in slow cooker. Top with chicken breasts.

2. Combine coconut milk, broth, curry powder, pepper sauce, if desired, salt and pepper in medium bowl. Pour over chicken. Cover; cook on LOW 6 to 8 hours.

3. About 30 minutes before serving, add peas to slow cooker.

4. Serve over hot cooked rice, if desired.

Makes 4 servings

Coconut Chicken Curry

Sandy's Mexican Chicken

    2 to 4 chicken breasts
    1 medium onion, cut into strips
    1 can (10¾ ounces) condensed cream of chicken soup
    1 can (10 ounces) Mexican-style tomatoes with green chilies, undrained
    1 package (8 ounces) American processed cheese food

1. Place all ingredients except cheese food in slow cooker. Cover; cook on LOW 6 to 8 hours or on HIGH 4 hours.

2. Break up chicken into pieces with spoon. Add cheese food; cook on HIGH until melted.

Makes 2 to 4 servings

Easy Slow Cooker Chicken and Gravy

    1 can (10¾ ounces) condensed cream of chicken soup
    6 to 8 chicken legs, breast halves or assorted pieces
    1 can (10¾ ounces) condensed cream of chicken Dijon soup *or* 2 cans
        (10¾ ounces each) cream of chicken soup

Pour 1 can chicken soup into slow cooker. Place chicken pieces over top. Pour chicken Dijon soup over chicken. Cover; cook on LOW 8 to 10 hours.

Makes 6 servings

Slow Cooker Turkey Breast

1 turkey breast (3 to 6 pounds)
Garlic powder
Paprika
Dried parsley flakes

Place turkey in slow cooker. Sprinkle with garlic powder, paprika and parsley to taste. Cover; cook on LOW 6 to 8 hours.

Makes 6 servings

Note: Don't add any liquid—the turkey makes its own juices.

Chicken Stew

4 to 5 cups chopped cooked chicken
1 can (28 ounces) whole tomatoes, undrained
2 large potatoes, cut in 1-inch pieces
1 large onion, chopped
½ pound okra, sliced
1 can (14 ounces) cream-style corn
½ cup ketchup
½ cup barbecue sauce

1. Combine chicken, tomatoes with juice, potatoes, onion and okra in slow cooker. Cover; cook on LOW 6 to 8 hours or until potatoes are tender.

2. Add corn, ketchup and barbecue sauce. Cover; cook on HIGH 30 minutes.

Makes 6 servings

Chinese Cashew Chicken

1 pound bean sprouts (fresh or canned)
2 cups sliced cooked chicken
1 can (10¾ ounces) condensed cream of mushroom soup
1 cup sliced celery
½ cup chopped green onion
1 can (4 ounces) mushroom pieces, drained
3 tablespoons butter
1 tablespoon soy sauce
1 cup cashews

1. Combine all ingredients except cashews in slow cooker. Cover; cook on LOW 4 to 6 hours or on HIGH 3 to 4 hours.

2. Just before serving, stir in cashews.

Makes 4 servings

SLOW COOKING SECRET

Clean the outside of the slow cooker electric unit by wiping clean with a damp paper towel or sponge. Do not put the unit in water.

Chinese Cashew Chicken

Chicken in Honey Sauce

4 to 6 boneless skinless chicken breasts
Salt
Black pepper
2 cups honey
1 cup soy sauce
½ cup ketchup
¼ cup oil
2 cloves garlic, minced
Sesame seeds

1. Place chicken in slow cooker; sprinkle with salt and pepper to taste.

2. Combine honey, soy sauce, ketchup, oil and garlic in large mixing bowl. Pour over chicken in slow cooker. Cover; cook on LOW 6 to 8 hours or on HIGH 3 to 4 hours.

3. Garnish with sesame seeds before serving.   *Makes 4 to 6 servings*

Chicken Reuben

1 tablespoon butter or margarine
2 large sweet onions (preferably Vidalia), chopped
4 to 6 chicken breasts
1 jar (28 ounces) sauerkraut, drained
4 to 6 slices Swiss cheese
1 bottle (16 ounces) Thousand Island salad dressing

1. Heat butter in large skillet over medium-low heat. Add onion and cook until tender.

2. Place half of chicken breasts in slow cooker. Top with half of onion mixture, half of sauerkraut, half of cheese slices and half of salad dressing. Repeat layers. Cover; cook on LOW 6 to 8 hours.

Makes 4 to 6 servings

SLOW COOKING SECRET

Be sure to clean the crockery insert completely between uses. Clean in the dishwasher if the insert is dishwasher-safe. Check the manufacturer's instructions.

MEATLESS MEALS

Mushroom Barley Stew

    1 tablespoon olive oil
    1 medium onion, finely chopped
    1 cup chopped carrots (about 2 carrots)
    1 clove garlic, minced
    1 cup pearled barley
    1 cup dried wild mushrooms, broken into pieces
    1 teaspoon salt
    ½ teaspoon black pepper
    ½ teaspoon dried thyme leaves
    5 cups vegetable broth

1. Heat oil in medium skillet over medium-high heat. Add onion, carrots and garlic; cook and stir 5 minutes or until tender. Place into slow cooker.

2. Add barley, mushrooms, salt, pepper and thyme. Sir in broth. Cover; cook on LOW 6 to 7 hours. Adjust seasonings, if desired.   *Makes 4 to 6 servings*

Variation: To turn this thick robust stew into a soup, add 2 to 3 additional cups of broth. Cook the same length of time.

Mushroom Barley Stew

Layered Mexican-Style Casserole

2 cans (15½ ounces each) hominy, drained
1 can (15 ounces) black beans, rinsed and drained
1 can (14½ ounces) diced tomatoes with garlic, basil and oregano, undrained
1 cup thick and chunky salsa
1 can (6 ounces) tomato paste
½ teaspoon ground cumin
3 large (about 9-inch diameter) flour tortillas
2 cups (8 ounces) shredded Monterey Jack cheese
¼ cup sliced black olives

1. Prepare foil handles (see below.) Place into slow cooke to make lifting of tortilla stack easier. Spray slow cooker with nonstick cooking spray.

2. Combine hominy, beans, tomatoes with juice, salsa, tomato paste and cumin in large bowl.

3. Press one tortilla in the bottom of slow cooker. (Edges of tortilla may turn up slightly.) Top with one third of the hominy mixture and one third of cheese. Repeat layers. Press remaining tortilla on top. Top with remaining hominy mixture. Set aside remaining cheese.

4. Cover; cook on LOW 6 to 8 hours. Sprinkle with remaining cheese and olives. Cover, let stand 5 minutes. Pull out with foil handles. *Makes 6 servings*

Note: Hominy is corn that has been treated with slaked lime to remove the germ and hull. It can be found with the canned vegetables in most supermarkets.

Foil Handles: Tear off three 18×2-inch strips of heavy foil or use regular foil folded to double thickness. Crisscross foil strips in spoke design as shown on page 7.

Layered Mexican-Style Casserole

Caribbean Sweet Potato & Bean Stew

    2 medium sweet potatoes (about 1 pound), peeled and cut into 1-inch cubes
    2 cups frozen cut green beans
    1 can (15 ounces) black beans, rinsed and drained
    1 can (14½ ounces) vegetable broth
    1 small onion, sliced
    2 teaspoons Caribbean or Jamaican jerk seasoning
    ½ teaspoon dried thyme leaves
    ¼ teaspoon ground cinnamon
    ¼ teaspoon salt
    ⅓ cup slivered almonds, toasted*
       Hot pepper sauce (optional)

To toast almonds, spread in single layer on baking sheet. Bake in preheated 350°F oven 8 to 10 minutes or until golden brown, stirring frequently.

1. Combine all ingredients except almonds and hot pepper sauce in slow cooker. Cover; cook on LOW 5 to 6 hours or until vegetables are tender.

2. Adjust seasonings. Serve with almonds and hot pepper sauce, if desired.

Makes 4 servings

SLOW COOKING SECRET

Leave the peel on slow-cooked vegetables to keep the shape and nutrients. Scrub the skins of potatoes and carrots, then chop and add to the slow cooker.

Caribbean Sweet Potato & Bean Stew

Three Pepper Pasta Sauce

1 *each* red, yellow and green bell pepper, cut into 1-inch pieces
2 cans (14½ ounces each) diced tomatoes, undrained
1 cup chopped onion
1 can (6 ounces) tomato paste
4 cloves garlic, minced
2 tablespoons olive oil
1 teaspoon dried basil leaves
1 teaspoon dried oregano leaves
½ teaspoon salt
¼ teaspoon red pepper flakes or ground black pepper
   Hot cooked pasta
   Shredded Parmesan or Romano cheese

1. Combine all ingredients except pasta and cheese in slow cooker. Cover; cook on LOW 7 to 8 hours or until vegetables are tender.

2. Adjust seasonings, if desired. Serve with pasta and cheese.   *Makes 4 to 6 servings*

Helpful Hint: 3 cups mixed bell pepper chunks from a salad bar may be substituted for peppers.

Three Pepper Pasta Sauce

Southwestern Corn and Beans

1 tablespoon olive oil
1 large onion, diced
1 or 2 jalapeño peppers,* diced
1 clove garlic, minced
2 cans (16 ounces) light red kidney beans, rinsed and drained
1 bag (16 ounces) frozen corn
1 can (14½ ounces) diced tomatoes, undrained
1 green bell pepper, cut into 1-inch pieces
2 teaspoons medium-hot chili powder
¾ teaspoon salt
½ teaspoon ground cumin
½ teaspoon black pepper
1 carton (8 ounces) plain yogurt (optional)
   Sliced black olives (optional)

*Jalapeño peppers can sting and irritate the skin; wear rubber gloves when handling peppers and do not touch eyes. Wash hands after handling.

1. Heat oil in medium skillet over medium heat. Add onion, jalapeño pepper and garlic; cook 5 minutes. Add onion mixture, kidney beans, corn, tomatoes with juice, bell pepper, chili powder, salt, cumin and black pepper to slow cooker. Cover; cook on LOW 7 to 8 hours.

2. Spoon corn and beans into bowls. Serve with yogurt and black olives, if desired.

Makes 6 servings

Serving Suggestion: For a party, spoon this colorful vegetarian dish into hollowed-out bread bowls.

Southwestern Corn and Beans

South-of-the-Border Macaroni & Cheese

    5 cups cooked rotini pasta
    2 cups (8 ounces) cubed American cheese
    1 can (12 ounces) evaporated milk
    1 cup (4 ounces) cubed sharp Cheddar cheese
    1 can (4 ounces) diced green chilies, drained
    2 teaspoons chili powder
    2 medium tomatoes, seeded and chopped
    5 green onions, sliced

1. Combine all ingredients, except tomatoes and onions in slow cooker; mix well. Cover; cook on HIGH 2 hours, stirring twice.

2. Stir in tomatoes and green onions; continue cooking until hot.   *Makes 4 servings*

Simmered Red Beans & Rice

    2 cans (15 ounces each) red beans, undrained
    1 can (14½ ounces) diced tomatoes, undrained
    ½ cup chopped celery
    ½ cup chopped green bell pepper
    ½ cup chopped green onions with tops
    2 cloves garlic, minced
    1 to 2 teaspoon hot pepper sauce
    1 teaspoon Worcestershire sauce
    1 bay leaf
       Hot cooked rice

1. Combine all ingredients except rice in slow cooker. Cover and cook on LOW 4 to 6 hours or on HIGH 2 to 3 hours. Remove and discard bay leaf.

2. Mash mixture slightly in slow cooker with potato masher until mixture thickens. Continue to cook on HIGH an additional 30 to 60 minutes. Serve over rice.   *Makes 6 (1-cup) servings*

South-of-the-Border Macaroni & Cheese

Southwestern Stuffed Peppers

    4 green bell peppers
    1 can (16 ounces) black beans, rinsed and drained
    1 cup (4 ounces) shredded Monterey Jack cheese with jalapeño peppers
    ¾ cup medium salsa
    ½ cup frozen corn
    ½ cup chopped green onions with tops
    ⅓ cup uncooked long grain converted rice
    1 teaspoon chili powder
    ½ teaspoon ground cumin
       Sour cream (optional)

1. Cut thin slice off top of each bell pepper. Carefully remove seeds, leaving pepper whole.

2. Combine remaining ingredients except sour cream in medium bowl. Spoon filling evenly into each pepper. Place peppers in slow cooker. Cover; cook on LOW 4 to 6 hours. Serve with dollop of sour cream, if desired.   *Makes 4 servings*

Mexican-Style Rice and Cheese

    1 can (16 ounces) Mexican-style beans
    1 can (14½ ounces) diced tomatoes with jalapeños, undrained
 1½ cups uncooked long-grain converted rice
    1 large onion, finely chopped
    ½ package (4 ounces) cream cheese
    3 cloves garlic, minced
    2 cups (8 ounces) shredded Monterey Jack or Colby cheese, divided

1. Mix all ingredients thoroughly except 1 cup shredded cheese. Pour mixture into well-greased slow cooker. Cover; cook on LOW 6 to 9 hours.

2. Just before serving, sprinkle with remaining 1 cup shredded cheese.

Makes 6 to 8 servings

Vegetarian Sausage Rice

2 cups chopped green bell peppers
1 can (15½ ounces) dark kidney beans, rinsed and drained
1 can (14½ ounces) diced tomatoes with green bell peppers and onions, undrained
1 cup chopped onion
1 cup sliced celery
1 cup water, divided
¾ cup uncooked long grain rice
1¼ teaspoons salt
1 teaspoon hot pepper sauce
½ teaspoon dried thyme leaves
½ teaspoon red pepper flakes
3 bay leaves
1 package (8-ounces) vegetable protein breakfast patties, thawed
2 tablespoons extra virgin olive oil
½ cup chopped fresh parsley leaves
Additional hot pepper sauce (optional)

1. Combine bell peppers, beans, tomatoes with juice, onion, celery, ½ cup water, rice, salt, pepper sauce, thyme, pepper flakes and bay leaves in slow cooker. Cover; cook on LOW 4 to 5 hours.

2. Dice breakfast patties. Heat oil in large nonstick skillet over medium-high heat. Add patties; cook 2 minutes or until lightly browned, scraping bottom of skillet occasionally.

3. Place patties in slow cooker. *Do not stir.* Add remaining ½ cup water to skillet; bring to a boil over high heat 1 minute, scraping up bits on bottom of skillet. Add liquid and parsley to slow cooker; stir gently to blend. Serve immediately with additional hot pepper sauce, if desired.

Makes 8 cups

Broccoli & Cheese Strata

 2 cups chopped broccoli florets
 4 slices firm white bread, ½-inch thick
 4 teaspoons butter
1½ cups (6 ounces) shredded Cheddar cheese
1½ cups low-fat (1%) milk
 3 eggs
 ½ teaspoon salt
 ½ teaspoon hot pepper sauce
 ⅛ teaspoon black pepper

1. Cook broccoli in boiling water 10 minutes or until tender; drain.

2. Spread one side of each bread slice with 1 teaspoon butter. Arrange 2 slices bread, buttered sides up, in greased 1-quart casserole that will fit in slow cooker. Layer cheese, broccoli and remaining 2 bread slices, buttered sides down.

3. Beat milk, eggs, salt, pepper sauce and black pepper in medium bowl. Gradually pour over bread.

4. Place small wire rack in 5-quart slow cooker. Pour in 1 cup water. Place casserole on rack. Cover; cook on HIGH 3 hours.   *Makes 4 servings*

Broccoli & Cheese Strata

Vegetarian Chili

  1 tablespoon vegetable oil
  1 cup finely chopped onion
  1 cup chopped red bell pepper
  2 tablespoons minced jalapeño pepper*
  1 clove garlic, minced
  1 can (28 ounces) crushed tomatoes, undrained
  1 can (14½ ounces) black beans, rinsed and drained
  1 can (14 ounces) garbanzo beans, rinsed and drained
½ cup corn
¼ cup tomato paste
  1 teaspoon sugar
  1 teaspoon ground cumin
  1 teaspoon dried basil leaves
  1 teaspoon chili powder
¼ teaspoon black pepper
    Sour cream and shredded Cheddar cheese (optional)

*Jalapeño peppers can sting and irritate the skin; wear rubber gloves when handling peppers and do not touch eyes. Wash hands after handling.

1. Heat oil in large nonstick skillet over medium-high heat until hot. Add onion, bell pepper, jalapeño pepper and garlic; cook and stir 5 minutes or until vegetables are tender.

2. Transfer vegetables to slow cooker. Add remaining ingredients except sour cream and cheese; mix well. Cover; cook on LOW 4 to 5 hours. Garnish with sour cream and cheese, if desired.

Makes 4 servings

Vegetarian Chili

Bean Ragoût
with Cilantro-Cornmeal Dumplings

Filling

    2 cans (14½ ounces each) diced tomatoes, undrained

    1 can (15½ ounces) pinto or kidney beans, rinsed and drained

    1 can (15½ ounces) black beans, rinsed and drained

 1½ cups chopped red bell pepper

    1 large onion, chopped

    2 small zucchini, sliced

    ½ cup chopped green bell pepper

    ½ cup chopped celery

    1 poblano chili pepper,* seeded and chopped

    2 cloves garlic, minced

    3 tablespoons chili powder

    2 teaspoons ground cumin

    1 teaspoon dried oregano leaves

    ¼ teaspoon salt

    ⅛ teaspoon black pepper

Topping

    ¼ cup all-purpose flour

    ¼ cup yellow cornmeal

    ½ teaspoon baking powder

    ¼ teaspoon salt

    1 tablespoon vegetable shortening

    2 tablespoons shredded Cheddar cheese

    2 teaspoons minced fresh cilantro

    ¼ cup milk

Bean Ragoût with Cilantro-Cornmeal Dumplings

1. Combine tomatoes with juice, beans, red bell pepper, onion, zucchini, green bell pepper, celery, poblano pepper, garlic, chili powder, cumin, oregano, ¼ teaspoon salt and black pepper in slow cooker; mix well. Cover; cook on LOW 7 to 8 hours.

2. Prepare dumplings 1 hour before serving. Mix flour, cornmeal, baking powder and ¼ teaspoon salt in medium bowl. Cut in shortening with pastry blender or two knives until mixture resembles coarse crumbs. Stir in cheese and cilantro. Pour milk into flour mixture. Blend just until dry ingredients are moistened. Turn slow cooker to HIGH. Drop dumplings by level tablespoonfuls (larger dumplings will not cook properly) on top of ragoût. Cover; cook 1 hour or until toothpick inserted into dumpling comes out clean.   *Makes 6 servings*

Hearty Lentil Stew

1 cup dried lentils, rinsed and drained
1 package (16 ounces) frozen green beans
2 cups cauliflower florets
1 cup chopped onion
1 cup baby carrots, cut in half crosswise
3 cups fat-free reduced-sodium chicken broth
2 teaspoons ground cumin
¾ teaspoon ground ginger
1 can (15 ounces) chunky tomato sauce with garlic and herbs
½ cup dry-roasted peanuts

1. Place lentils in slow cooker. Top with green beans, cauliflower, onion and carrots. Combine broth, cumin and ginger in large bowl; mix well. Pour mixture over vegetables. Cover; cook on LOW 9 to 11 hours.

2. Stir in tomato sauce. Cover; cook on LOW 10 minutes. Ladle stew into bowls. Sprinkle peanuts evenly over each serving.

Makes 6 servings

SLOW COOKING SECRET

Cut dense vegetables like potatoes and carrots into pieces no larger than 1 inch thick to make sure they cook through.

Hearty Lentil Stew

Vegetable Pasta Sauce

    2 cans (14½ ounces each) diced tomatoes, undrained
    1 can (14½ ounces) whole tomatoes, undrained
1½ cups sliced mushrooms
    1 medium red bell pepper, diced
    1 medium green bell pepper, diced
    1 small yellow squash, cut into ¼-inch slices
    1 small zucchini, cut into ¼-inch slices
    1 can (6 ounces) tomato paste
    4 green onions, sliced
    2 tablespoons dried Italian seasoning
    1 tablespoon chopped fresh parsley
    3 cloves garlic, minced
    1 teaspoon salt
    1 teaspoon red pepper flakes (optional)
    1 teaspoon black pepper
    Hot cooked pasta
    Parmesan cheese and fresh basil for garnish (optional)

1. Combine all ingredients except pasta and garnishes in slow cooker, stirring thoroughly to combine. Cover; cook on LOW 6 to 8 hours.

2. Serve over cooked pasta. Garnish with Parmesan cheese and fresh basil, if desired.

Makes 4 to 6 servings

Vegetable Pasta Sauce

Garden Potato Casserole

1¼ pounds baking potatoes, unpeeled and sliced
1 small green or red bell pepper, thinly sliced
¼ cup finely chopped yellow onion
2 tablespoons butter, cut into ⅛-inch pieces, divided
½ teaspoon salt
½ teaspoon dried thyme leaves
Black pepper to taste
1 small yellow squash, thinly sliced
1 cup (4 ounces) shredded sharp Cheddar cheese

1. Place potatoes, bell pepper, onion, 1 tablespoon butter, salt, thyme and black pepper in slow cooker; mix well. Evenly layer squash over potato mixture; add remaining 1 tablespoon butter. Cover; cook on LOW 7 hours or on HIGH 4 hours.

2. Remove potato mixture to serving bowl. Sprinkle with cheese and let stand 2 to 3 minutes or until cheese melts.

Makes 5 servings

SLOW COOKING SECRET
Sprinkle a small amount of snipped fresh herbs over slow cooker dishes for a quick simple flavor enhancer.

Garden Potato Casserole

Potato Casserole with Creamy Cheese Sauce

2 pounds russet potatoes, sliced
2 medium yellow squash, cut into ¼-inch slices
1 cup chopped onions
1 cup chopped red bell pepper
⅓ cup water
2 tablespoons butter
¾ teaspoon dried thyme leaves
¾ teaspoon salt
¼ teaspoon black pepper
⅛ teaspoon ground red pepper
½ cup half and half
8 slices processed American cheese

1. Place all ingredients into slow cooker except half and half and cheese in the order listed above. Cover; cook on HIGH 3 hours.

2. Remove vegetables with slotted spoon and place in serving bowl. Stir half and half and cheese into slow cooker. Cover; cook 5 minutes or until cheese melts. Whisk until well blended; pour over vegetables.

Makes 8 cups

Slow Cooker Veggie Stew

1 tablespoon vegetable oil
⅔ cup sliced carrots
½ cup diced onion
2 cloves garlic, chopped
2 cans (14 ounces each) fat-free vegetable broth
1½ cups chopped green cabbage
½ cup cut green beans
½ cup diced zucchini
1 tablespoon tomato paste
½ teaspoon dried basil leaves
½ teaspoon dried oregano leaves
¼ teaspoon salt

1. Heat oil in medium skillet over medium-high heat. Add carrots, onion and garlic. Cook and stir until tender.

2. Place carrot mixture and remaining ingredients in slow cooker. Cover; cook on LOW 8 to 10 hours or on HIGH 3 hours.

Makes 4 to 6 serving

SLOW COOKING SECRET

For easier preparation, cut up vegetables for the slow cooker the night before. Wrap tightly and refrigerate until ready to use.

Hot & Juicy Sandwiches

Slow-Cooked Kielbasa in a Bun

- 1 pound kielbasa, cut into 4 (4- to 5-inch) pieces
- 1 large onion, thinly sliced
- 1 large green bell pepper, cut into strips
- ¼ teaspoon salt
- ¼ teaspoon dried thyme leaves
- ¼ teaspoon black pepper
- ½ cup chicken broth
- 4 hoagie rolls, split

1. Brown kielbasa in nonstick skillet over medium-high heat 3 to 4 minutes. Place kielbasa into slow cooker. Add onion, bell pepper, salt, thyme and pepper. Stir in chicken broth. Cover; cook on LOW 7 to 8 hours.

2. Place kielbasa in rolls. Top with portion of onion and bell pepper. Serve with favorite condiments.

Makes 4 servings

Serving Suggestion: For zesty flavor, top sandwiches with pickled peppers and a dollop of mustard.

Slow-Cooked Kielbasa in a Bun

Shredded Apricot Pork Sandwiches

2 medium onions, thinly sliced
1 cup apricot preserves
½ cup packed dark brown sugar
½ cup barbecue sauce
¼ cup cider vinegar
2 tablespoons Worcestershire sauce
½ teaspoon red pepper flakes
1 (4-pound) boneless pork loin roast, trimmed of fat
¼ cup cold water
2 tablespoons cornstarch
1 tablespoon grated fresh ginger
1 teaspoon salt
1 teaspoon black pepper
10 to 12 sesame or onion rolls, toasted

1. Combine onions, preserves, brown sugar, barbecue sauce, vinegar, Worcestershire sauce and pepper flakes in small bowl. Place pork roast into slow cooker. Pour apricot mixture over roast. Cover; cook on LOW 8 to 9 hours.

2. Remove pork from cooking liquid to cutting board; cool slightly. Using 2 forks, shred pork into coarse shreds. Let liquid stand 5 minutes to allow fat to rise. Skim fat.

3. Combine water, cornstarch, ginger, salt and pepper; blend well. Whisk cornstarch mixture into slow cooker liquid. Cook on HIGH 15 to 30 minutes or until thickened.

4. Return shredded pork to slow cooker; mix well. Serve in toasted buns.

Makes 10 to 12 sandwiches

Variation: 1 (4-pound) pork shoulder roast, cut into pieces and trimmed of fat, may be substituted for pork loin roast.

Shredded Apricot Pork Sandwich

Hot & Juicy Reuben Sandwiches

1 mild-cure corned beef (1½ pounds)
2 cups sauerkraut, drained
½ cup beef broth
1 small onion, sliced
1 clove garlic, minced
¼ teaspoon caraway seeds
4 to 6 peppercorns
8 slices pumpernickel or rye bread
4 slices Swiss cheese
Mustard

1. Trim excess fat from corned beef. Place meat into slow cooker. Add sauerkraut, broth, onion, garlic, caraway seeds and peppercorns. Cover; cook on LOW 7 to 9 hours.

2. Remove beef from slow cooker. Cut across the grain into ¼-inch-thick slices. Divide evenly among 4 slices bread. Top each slice with ½ cup drained sauerkraut mixture and one slice cheese. Spread mustard on remaining 4 bread slices. Close sandwich. *Makes 4 servings*

Note: This two-fisted stack of corned beef, sauerkraut and melted Swiss cheese makes a glorious sandwich you'll serve often using slow-cooked corned beef.

Hot & Juicy Reuben Sandwich

Spicy Asian Pork Filling

1 boneless pork sirloin roast (3 pounds)
½ cup tamari or soy sauce
1 tablespoon chili garlic sauce or chili paste
2 teaspoons minced fresh ginger
2 tablespoons water
1 tablespoon cornstarch
2 teaspoons dark sesame oil

1. Cut roast into 2- to 3-inch chunks. Combine pork, tamari sauce, chili garlic sauce and ginger in slow cooker; mix well. Cover; cook on LOW 8 to 10 hours or until pork is fork tender.

2. Remove roast from cooking liquid; cool slightly. Trim and discard excess fat. Shred pork using 2 forks.

3. Let liquid stand 5 minutes to allow fat to rise. Skim off fat.

4. Blend water, cornstarch and sesame oil; whisk into liquid. Cook on HIGH until thickened. Add shredded meat to slow cooker; mix well. Cook 15 to 30 minutes or until hot.

Makes 5½ cups filling

Spicy Asian Pork Bundles: Place ¼ cup pork filling into large lettuce leaves. Wrap to enclose. Makes about 20 bundles.

Moo Shu Pork: Lightly spread plum sauce over warm small flour tortillas. Spoon ¼ cup pork filling and ¼ cup stir-fried vegetables into flour tortillas. Wrap to enclose. Serve immediately. Makes about 20 tortillas.

Brats in Beer

1½ pounds bratwurst links (about 5 or 6)
1 can or bottle (12 ounces) beer (not dark)
1 medium onion, thinly sliced
2 tablespoons brown sugar
2 tablespoons red wine or cider vinegar
    Mustard
5 to 6 rye or onion sandwich rolls

1. Place bratwurst, beer, onion, sugar and vinegar into slow cooker. Cover; cook on LOW 4 to 5 hours.

2. Remove bratwurst from cooking liquid. Serve with mustard in sandwich rolls.

Makes 5 to 6 servings

Helpful Hint: Choose a light-tasting beer for cooking brats. Hearty ales might leave the meat tasting slightly bitter.

Italian Beef

1 boneless beef chuck shoulder roast (5 to 6 pounds), cut in half
3½ cups water
4 medium green bell peppers, sliced
1 onion, sliced
3 tablespoons vinegar
1½ teaspoons salt
½ teaspoon black pepper
3 teaspoons caraway seeds
3 bay leaves
¼ teaspoon dried oregano leaves

Combine all ingredients in slow cooker. Cover; cook on LOW 8 to 12 hours or until very tender. Remove and discard bay leaves before serving.

Makes 8 to 10 servings

Serving Suggestion: Serve thinly sliced on buns with a small amount of juice.

Easy Beef Sandwiches

1 large onion, sliced
1 boneless beef bottom round roast (3 to 5 pounds)
1 cup water
1 envelope (1 ounce) au jus mix

Place onion slices in bottom of slow cooker; top with roast. Combine water and au jus mix in small bowl; pour over roast. Cover; cook on low 7 to 9 hours. *Makes 6 to 8 servings*

Serving Suggestion: Before serving, shred the beef. Serve on French bread with the liquid from the slow cooker. Top with provolone cheese for a fantastic sandwich.

Burgundy Beef Po' Boys with Dipping Sauce

1 boneless beef chuck shoulder or bottom round roast (3 pounds)
2 cups chopped onion
¼ cup red wine
3 tablespoons balsamic vinegar
1 tablespoon beef bouillon granules
1 tablespoon Worcestershire sauce
¾ teaspoon dried thyme leaves
½ teaspoon garlic powder
Italian rolls, warmed and split

1. Cut beef into 3 or 4 pieces; trim fat. Place onions on bottom of a slow cooker. Top with beef and remaining ingredients. Cover; cook on HIGH 8 to 10 hours or until beef is very tender.

2. Remove beef from cooking liquid; cool slightly. Trim and discard fat from beef. Using two forks, shred meat. Let cooking liquid stand 5 minutes to allow fat to rise. Skim off fat.

3. Spoon beef into rolls and serve liquid as dipping sauce. *Makes 6 to 8 sandwiches*

Easy Beef Sandwich

Chicken Enchilada Roll-Ups

1½ pounds boneless skinless chicken breasts
½ cup plus 2 tablespoons all-purpose flour, divided
½ teaspoon salt
2 tablespoons butter
1 cup chicken broth
1 small onion, diced
¼ to ½ cup canned jalapeño peppers, sliced
½ teaspoon dried oregano leaves
2 tablespoons cream or milk
6 flour tortillas (7 to 8 inches)
6 thin slices American cheese or American cheese with jalapeño peppers

1. Cut each chicken breast lengthwise into 2 or 3 strips. Combine ½ cup flour and salt in plastic food storage bag. Add chicken strips and shake to coat with flour mixture. Melt butter in large skillet over medium heat. Brown chicken strips in batches 2 to 3 minutes per side. Place chicken into slow cooker.

2. Add chicken broth to skillet and scrape up any browned bits. Pour broth mixture into slow cooker. Add onion, jalapeño peppers and oregano. Cover; cook on LOW 7 to 8 hours.

3. Combine remaining 2 tablespoons flour and cream in small bowl; stir to form paste. Stir into chicken mixture; cook on HIGH until thickened.

4. Spoon chicken mixture onto center of flour tortillas. Top with 1 cheese slice. Fold up tortillas and serve.   *Makes 6 servings*

Serving Suggestion: This rich creamy chicken mixture can also be served over cooked rice.

Chicken Enchilada Roll-Up

BBQ Beef Sandwiches

1 lean boneless beef chuck roast (about 3 pounds)
¼ cup ketchup
2 tablespoons brown sugar
2 tablespoons red wine vinegar
1 tablespoon Dijon mustard
1 tablespoon Worcestershire sauce
1 clove garlic, crushed
¼ teaspoon salt
¼ teaspoon liquid smoke flavoring
⅛ teaspoon black pepper
10 to 12 French rolls or sandwich buns

1. Place beef into slow cooker. Combine remaining ingredients except rolls in medium bowl; pour over meat. Cover; cook on LOW 8 to 9 hours.

2. Remove beef from slow cooker; shred with 2 forks. Combine beef with 1 cup sauce from slow cooker. Spoon meat and sauce mixture onto warmed rolls. Top with additional sauce, if desired. *Makes 10 to 12 servings*

Helpful Hint: This recipe can be prepared ahead of time. Place cooked filling in a covered storage container and refrigerate. Reheat filling in the microwave or on top of the stove.

BBQ Beef Sandwich

Shredded Beef Wraps

1 flank steak or skirt steak (1 to 1½ pounds)
1 cup beef broth
½ cup sun-dried tomatoes (not packed in oil), chopped
3 to 4 cloves garlic, minced
¼ teaspoon ground cumin
8 flour tortillas
   Toppings: shredded lettuce, diced tomatoes, shredded Monterey Jack cheese (optional)

1. Cut flank steak into quarters. Place flank steak, beef broth, tomatoes, garlic and cumin in slow cooker. Cover; cook on LOW 7 to 8 hours or until meat easily shreds.

2. Remove beef from slow cooker; shred beef with fork or cut into thin strips.

3. Place remaining juices from slow cooker in blender or food processor; blend until sauce is smooth.

4. Spoon meat onto tortillas with small amount of sauce. Add desired toppings. Fold up and serve. *Makes 4 servings*

Hot Chicken Baguettes

1 to 2 carrots, sliced
½ cup sliced celery
1 small onion, chopped
1 clove garlic, minced
¼ teaspoon dried oregano leaves
¼ teaspoon red pepper flakes
6 boneless skinless chicken thighs or breasts
¼ cup all-purpose flour
1 teaspoon salt
½ teaspoon black pepper
1 tablespoon vegetable oil
1 can (14½ ounces) chicken broth
6 small French bread baguettes, split and toasted
6 slices Swiss cheese (optional)

1. Place carrots, celery, onion, garlic, oregano and pepper flakes into slow cooker.

2. Trim visible fat from chicken. Combine flour, salt and black pepper in plastic food storage bag. Add chicken, 2 pieces at a time; shake to coat with flour mixture. Heat oil in large skillet over medium-high heat. Add chicken and brown about 2 minutes on each side.

3. Place chicken over vegetables in slow cooker; add chicken broth. Cover; cook on LOW 5 to 6 hours or until chicken is tender.

4. Place 1 piece chicken on bottom half of each baguette. Spoon 1 to 2 tablespoons broth mixture over chicken. Top with 1 slice cheese, if desired. Close baguette.   *Makes 6 servings*

Italian Combo Subs

1 tablespoon vegetable oil
1 pound round steak, sliced into thin strips
1 pound bulk Italian sausage
1 medium onion, thinly sliced
1 can (4 ounces) sliced mushrooms (optional)
1 green bell pepper, cut into strips
   Salt
   Black pepper
1 jar (25 ounces) spaghetti sauce
2 loaves Italian bread, cut into 1-inch-thick slices

1. Heat oil in large skillet over medium-high heat. Gently brown round steak strips; transfer to slow cooker. Drain excess fat from skillet.

2. In same skillet, brown Italian sausage until no longer pink. Drain excess fat. Add sausage to slow cooker.

3. Place onion, mushrooms, if desired and bell pepper over meat. Season with salt and black pepper to taste; top with spaghetti sauce. Cover; cook on LOW 4 to 6 hours.

4. Serve as a sandwich.

Makes 6 servings

Serving Suggestion: Top with freshly grated Parmesan cheese.

Italian Combo Sub

Easy Beefy Sandwiches

- **1 boneless beef rump roast (2 to 4 pounds)**
- **1 envelope (1 ounce) Italian salad dressing mix**
- **1 envelope (1 ounce) dried onion soup mix**
- **2 beef bouillon cubes**
- **2 tablespoons prepared yellow mustard**
-     **Garlic powder**
-     **Onion powder**
-     **Salt**
-     **Black pepper**
- **1 cup water**

Place roast, salad dressing mix, onion soup mix, bouillon cubes and mustard in slow cooker. Season to taste with garlic powder, onion powder, salt and pepper. Add water. Cover; cook on LOW 8 to 10 hours.   *Makes 6 to 8 servings*

Serving Suggestion: Slice roast and serve with provolone, mozzarella or Lorraine Swiss cheese on crusty rolls.

SLOW COOKING SECRET

Purchase cuts of meat that will fit the size of your slow cooker. It may be necessary to trim a large roast into 2 to 3 pieces. Choose lean cuts and trim off visible fat.

Easy Beefy Sandwich

Chorizo Burritos

    15 ounces chorizo, cut in bite-size pieces
     1 can (about 15 ounces) red beans, rinsed and drained
     1 can (14½ ounces) diced tomatoes, undrained
     1 can (11 ounces) corn, drained
     2 green or red bell peppers, cut in 1-inch pieces
     1 cup chicken broth
    ½ teaspoon ground cinnamon
    ½ teaspoon ground cumin
     8 to 10 flour tortillas, warmed
       Hot cooked rice
       Shredded Monterey Jack cheese or sour cream

1. Place all ingredients except tortillas, rice and cheese into slow cooker; mix well. Cover; cook on LOW 6 to 8 hours.

2. Spoon filling down centers of warm tortillas; top with rice and shredded cheese. Roll up and serve immediately. *Makes 5 to 6 servings*

Tavern Burger

     1 tablespoon vegetable oil
     2 pounds extra-lean ground beef
    ½ cup ketchup
    ¼ cup brown sugar
    ¼ cup yellow mustard
       Hamburger buns

1. Heat oil in large skillet over medium-low heat. Brown beef, stirring to break up meat. Drain excess fat.

2. Place beef and remaining ingredients into slow cooker; mix well. Cover; cook on LOW 4 to 6 hours. *Makes 8 servings*

Serving Suggestion: Serve a scoopful on a hamburger bun.

Mexican-Style Shredded Beef

   1 beef chuck shoulder roast (2½ to 3 pounds)
   1 tablespoon chili powder
   1 tablespoon ground cumin
   1 tablespoon ground coriander
   1 teaspoon salt
  ½ teaspoon ground red pepper
   1 cup salsa or picante sauce
   2 tablespoons water
   1 tablespoon cornstarch

1. Cut roast in half. Combine chili powder, cumin, coriander, salt and red pepper in a small bowl. Rub over beef. Place ¼ cup of salsa in slow cooker; top with one piece beef. Layer ¼ cup salsa, remaining beef and ½ cup salsa in slow cooker. Cover; cook on LOW 8 to 10 hours or until meat is tender.

2. Remove beef from cooking liquid; cool slightly. Trim and discard excess fat from beef. Using two forks, shred meat.

3. Let cooking liquid stand 5 minutes to allow fat to rise. Skim off fat. To thicken liquid blend water and cornstarch. Whisk into liquid. Cook on HIGH until thickened.

4. Return beef to slow cooker and cook 15 to 30 minutes until hot. Adjust seasonings, if desired.

5. Serve as meat filling for tacos, fajitas or burritos. Leftover mixture may be refrigerated up to 3 days or frozen up to 3 months. *Makes 5 cups filling*

HOME-STYLE SIDES

Winter Squash and Apples

 1 teaspoon salt
½ teaspoon black pepper
 1 butternut squash (about 2 pounds), peeled and seeded
 2 apples, cored and cut into slices
 1 medium onion, quartered and sliced
1½ tablespoons butter

1. Combine salt and pepper in small bowl; set aside.

2. Cut squash into 2-inch pieces and place into slow cooker. Add apples and onion. Sprinkle with salt mixture; stir well. Cover; cook on LOW 6 to 7 hours.

3. Just before serving, stir in butter and season with additional salt and pepper to taste.

Makes 4 to 6 servings

Variation: Add ¼ to ½ cup brown sugar and ½ teaspoon cinnamon with butter; mix well.

Winter Squash and Apples

Risotto-Style Peppered Rice

 1 cup uncooked converted long grain rice
 1 medium green bell pepper, chopped
 1 medium red bell pepper, chopped
 1 cup chopped onion
 ½ teaspoon ground turmeric
 ⅛ teaspoon ground red pepper (optional)
 1 can (14½ ounces) fat-free chicken broth
 4 ounces Monterey Jack cheese with jalapeño peppers, cubed
 ½ cup milk
 ¼ cup butter, cubed
 1 teaspoon salt

1. Place rice, bell peppers, onion, turmeric and red pepper, if desired, into slow cooker. Stir in broth. Cover; cook on LOW 4 to 5 hours or until rice is done.

2. Stir in cheese, milk, butter and salt; fluff rice with fork. Cover; cook on LOW 5 minutes or until cheese melts. *Makes 4 to 6 servings*

Scalloped Tomatoes & Corn

 1 can (15 ounces) cream-style corn
 1 can (14½ ounces) diced tomatoes, undrained
 ¾ cup saltine cracker crumbs
 1 egg, slightly beaten
 2 teaspoons sugar
 ¾ teaspoon black pepper

1. Combine all ingredients in slow cooker; mix well. Cover; cook on LOW 4 to 6 hours.
Makes 4 to 6 servings

Risotto-Style Peppered Rice

Red Cabbage and Apples

- 1 small head red cabbage, cored and thinly sliced
- 3 medium apples, peeled and grated
- ¾ cup sugar
- ½ cup red wine vinegar
- 1 teaspoon ground cloves
- 1 cup crisp-cooked and crumbled bacon (optional)

Combine cabbage, apples, sugar, red wine vinegar and cloves in slow cooker. Cover; cook on HIGH 6 hours, stirring after 3 hours. Sprinkle with bacon, if desired.   *Makes 4 to 6 servings*

Delicious Parsnip Casserole

- 2 pounds parsnips, peeled and sliced
- 1 cup (4 ounces) shredded sharp Cheddar cheese
- ⅔ cup evaporated low-fat milk
- ¼ cup saltine cracker crumbs
- 6 slices bacon, crisp-cooked and crumbled
- 1 egg, well beaten
- 1½ teaspoons prepared horseradish
- 1 teaspoon salt
- ¼ teaspoon black pepper

1. Cook parsnips in boiling water about 15 minutes or until tender; drain well. Mash with potato masher until creamy. Add remaining ingredients; blend well.

2. Spoon mixture into buttered slow cooker. Cover; cook on LOW 4 to 5 hours.

Makes 4 to 6 servings

Red Cabbage and Apples

Five-Bean Casserole

2 medium onions, chopped
8 ounces bacon, diced
2 cloves garlic, minced
½ cup packed brown sugar
½ cup cider vinegar
1 teaspoon salt
1 teaspoon dry mustard
¼ teaspoon black pepper
2 cans (about 16 ounces each) kidney beans, rinsed and drained
1 can (about 16 ounces) chick-peas, rinsed and drained
1 can (about 16 ounces) butter beans, rinsed and drained
1 can (about 16 ounces) Great Northern or cannellini beans, rinsed and drained
1 can (about 16 ounces) baked beans

1. Cook and stir onions, bacon and garlic in large skillet over medium heat until onions are tender; drain. Stir in brown sugar, vinegar, salt, mustard and pepper. Simmer over low heat 15 minutes.

2. Combine beans in slow cooker. Spoon onion mixture evenly over top. Cover; cook on HIGH 3 to 4 hours or on LOW 6 to 8 hours.

Makes 16 servings

Parmesan Potato Wedges

   2 pounds red potatoes, cut into ½-inch wedges
   ¼ cup finely chopped yellow onion
1½ teaspoons dried oregano leaves
   ½ teaspoon salt
      Black pepper to taste
   2 tablespoons butter, cut into ⅛-inch pieces
   ¼ cup (1 ounce) grated Parmesan cheese

Layer potatoes, onion, oregano, salt, pepper and butter in slow cooker. Cover; cook on HIGH 4 hours. Transfer potatoes to serving platter and sprinkle with cheese. *Makes 6 servings*

SLOW COOKING SECRET

When adapting your own recipes for the slow cooker, use processed cheese or cheese spreads if heating cheese for a long time.

Mediterranean Red Potatoes

    3 medium red potatoes, cut in half lengthwise, then crosswise into pieces
    ⅔ cup fresh or frozen pearl onions
       Nonstick garlic-flavored cooking spray
    ¾ teaspoon dried Italian seasoning
    ¼ teaspoon black pepper
    1 small tomato, seeded and chopped
    2 ounces (½ cup) feta cheese, crumbled
    2 tablespoons chopped black olives

1. Place potatoes and onions in 1½-quart soufflé dish. Spray potatoes and onions with cooking spray; toss to coat. Add Italian seasoning and pepper; mix well. Cover dish tightly with foil.

2. Tear off 3 (18×3-inch) strips of heavy-duty aluminum foil. Cross strips to resemble wheel spokes as shown on page 7. Place soufflé dish in center of strips. Pull foil strips up and over dish and place dish into slow cooker.

3. Pour hot water into slow cooker to about 1½ inches from top of soufflé dish. Cover; cook on LOW 7 to 8 hours.

4. Use foil handles to lift dish out of slow cooker. Stir tomato, feta cheese and olives into potato mixture.   *Makes 4 servings*

Mediterranean Red Potatoes

Spanish Paella-Style Rice

   2 cans (14½ ounces each) chicken broth
1½ cups converted long grain rice, uncooked (not quick cooking or instant rice)
   1 small red bell pepper, diced
  ⅓ cup dry white wine or water
  ½ teaspoon powdered saffron *or* ½ teaspoon turmeric
  ⅛ teaspoon red pepper flakes
  ½ cup frozen peas, thawed
    Salt

1. Combine broth, rice, bell pepper, wine, saffron and pepper flakes in slow cooker; mix well. Cover; cook on LOW 4 hours or until liquid is absorbed.

2. Stir in peas. Cover; cook on LOW 15 to 30 minutes or until peas are hot. Season with salt.

Makes 6 servings

Note: Paella is a Spanish dish of saffron-flavored rice combined with a variety of meats, seafood and vegetables. Paella is traditionally served in a wide-shallow dish.

Variation: Add ½ cup cooked chicken, ham or shrimp or quartered marinated artichokes, drained, with peas.

Spanish Paella-Style Rice

Sweet-Spiced Sweet Potatoes

2 pounds sweet potatoes, peeled and cut into ½-inch pieces
¼ cup packed dark brown sugar
1 teaspoon ground cinnamon
½ teaspoon ground nutmeg
⅛ teaspoon salt
2 tablespoons butter, cut into ⅛-inch pieces
1 teaspoon vanilla

Combine all ingredients except butter and vanilla in slow cooker; mix well. Cover; cook on LOW 7 hours or cook on HIGH 4 hours. Add butter and vanilla; stir to blend.

Makes 4 servings

Polenta-Style Corn Casserole

1 can (14½ ounces) chicken broth
½ cup cornmeal
1 can (7 ounces) corn, drained
1 can (4 ounces) green chilies, drained
¼ cup diced red bell pepper
½ teaspoon salt
¼ teaspoon black pepper
1 cup shredded Cheddar cheese

1. Pour chicken broth into slow cooker. Whisk in cornmeal. Add corn, chilies, bell pepper, salt and pepper. Cover; cook on LOW 4 to 5 hours or on HIGH 2 to 3 hours.

2. Stir in cheese. Continue cooking, uncovered, 15 to 30 minutes or until cheese melts.

Makes 6 servings

Serving Suggestion: Divide cooked corn mixture into lightly greased individual ramekins or spread in pie plate; cover and refrigerate. Serve at room temperature or warm in oven or microwave.

Sweet-Spiced Sweet Potatoes

Busy-Day Rice

    2 cups water
    1 cup converted white rice
    2 tablespoons butter
    1 tablespoon dried minced onions
    1 tablespoon dried parsley flakes
    2 teaspoons chicken bouillon granules
        Dash ground red pepper (optional)

Combine all ingredients in slow cooker; mix well. Cover; cook on HIGH 2 hours or until rice is tender. *Makes 4 servings*

Variation: During the last 30 minutes of cooking, add ½ cup green peas, tiny broccoli florets, corn or diced carrots.

No-Fuss Macaroni & Cheese

    2 cups (about 8 ounces) uncooked elbow macaroni
    4 ounces light pasteurized processed cheese, cubed
    1 cup (4 ounces) shredded mild Cheddar cheese
    ½ teaspoon salt
    ⅛ teaspoon black pepper
    1½ cups fat-free (skim) milk

Combine macaroni, cheeses, salt and pepper in slow cooker. Pour milk over top. Cover; cook on LOW 2 to 3 hours, stirring after 20 to 30 minutes. *Makes 6 to 8 servings*

Variation: Stir in sliced hot dogs or desired vegetable.

Helpful Hint: As with all macaroni and cheese dishes, as it sits, the cheese sauce thickens and begins to dry out. If it dries out, stir in a little extra milk and heat through. Do not cook longer than 4 hours.

Note: This is a simple way to make macaroni and cheese without taking the time to boil water and cook noodles. Kids can even make this one on their own.

Sweet Potato & Pecan Casserole

    1 can (40 ounces) sweet potatoes, drained and mashed
    ½ cup apple juice
    ⅓ cup butter, melted
    ½ teaspoon salt
    ½ teaspoon ground cinnamon
    ¼ teaspoon black pepper
    2 eggs, beaten
    ⅓ cup chopped pecans
    ⅓ cup brown sugar
    2 tablespoons all-purpose flour
    2 tablespoons butter, melted

1. Lightly grease slow cooker. Combine sweet potatoes, apple juice, ⅓ cup butter, salt, cinnamon and pepper in large bowl. Beat in eggs. Place mixture into prepared slow cooker.

2. Combine pecans, brown sugar, flour and 2 tablespoons butter in small bowl. Spread over sweet potatoes. Cover; cook on HIGH 3 to 4 hours.   *Makes 6 to 8 servings*

Note: This casserole is excellent to make for the holidays.

SLOW COOKING SECRET

Using the slow cooker when preparing large meals frees up your oven for other dishes. The cook can also prepare slow cooker dishes in advance, allowing time for other last minute meal preparations.

Spinach Spoonbread

1 package (10 ounces) frozen chopped spinach, thawed and squeezed dry
1 red bell pepper, diced
4 eggs, lightly beaten
1 cup cottage cheese
1 package (5½ ounces) cornbread mix
6 green onions, sliced
½ cup butter, melted
1¼ teaspoons seasoned salt

1. Lightly grease slow cooker; preheat on HIGH.

2. Combine all ingredients in large bowl; mix well. Pour batter into preheated slow cooker. Cook, covered with lid slightly ajar to allow excess moisture to escape, on HIGH 1¾ to 2 hours or on LOW 3 to 4 hours or until edges are golden and knife inserted in center of bread comes out clean.

3. Serve bread spooned from slow cooker, or loosen edges and bottom with knife and invert onto plate. Cut into wedges to serve.

Makes 8 servings

SLOW COOKING SECRET

Avoid using completely frozen foods in the slow cooker. Thaw in the microwave before adding to the slow cooker.

Spinach Spoonbread

Scalloped Potatoes and Parsnips

    6 tablespoons unsalted butter
    3 tablespoons all-purpose flour
1¾ cups heavy cream
    2 teaspoons dry mustard
1½ teaspoons salt
    1 teaspoon dried thyme leaves
    ½ teaspoon black pepper
    2 baking potatoes, cut in half lengthwise, then in ¼-inch slices crosswise
    2 parsnips, cut into ¼-inch slices
    1 onion, chopped
    2 cups (8 ounces) shredded sharp Cheddar cheese

1. Melt butter in medium saucepan over medium-high heat. Add flour and whisk constantly 3 to 5 minutes. Slowly whisk in cream, mustard, salt, thyme and pepper. Stir until smooth.

2. Place potatoes, parsnips and onion into slow cooker. Add cream sauce. Cover; cook on LOW 7 hours or on HIGH 3½ hours or until potatoes are tender.

3. Stir in cheese. Cover until cheese melts.

Makes 4 to 6 servings

Scalloped Potatoes and Parsnips

Green Bean Casserole

   2 packages (10 ounces each) frozen green beans, thawed
   1 can (10½ ounces) condensed cream of mushroom soup
   1 tablespoon chopped fresh parsley
   1 tablespoon chopped roasted red peppers
   1 teaspoon dried sage leaves
   ½ teaspoon salt
   ½ teaspoon black pepper
   ¼ teaspoon ground nutmeg
   ½ cup toasted slivered almonds

Combine all ingredients except almonds in slow cooker. Cover; cook on LOW 3 to 4 hours. Sprinkle with almonds.   *Makes 4 to 6 servings*

Blue Cheese Potatoes

   2 pounds red potatoes, peeled and cut into ½-inch pieces
1¼ cups chopped green onions, divided
   2 tablespoons olive oil, divided
   1 teaspoon dried basil leaves
   ½ teaspoon salt
   ¼ teaspoon black pepper
   2 ounces crumbled blue cheese

1. Layer potatoes, 1 cup onions, 1 tablespoon oil, basil, salt and pepper in slow cooker. Cover; cook on LOW 7 hours or on HIGH 4 hours.

2. Gently stir in cheese and remaining 1 tablespoon oil. If slow cooker is on LOW turn to HIGH; cook an additional 5 minutes to allow flavors to blend. Transfer potatoes to serving platter and top with remaining ¼ cup onions.   *Makes 5 servings*

Green Bean Casserole

Cheesy Broccoli Casserole

     2 packages (10 ounces each) chopped broccoli, thawed
     1 can (10¾ ounces) condensed cream of potato soup
  1¼ cups shredded sharp Cheddar cheese, divided
     ¼ cup minced onions
     1 teaspoon hot pepper sauce
     1 cup crushed saltine crackers or potato chips

1. Lightly grease slow cooker. Combine broccoli, soup, 1 cup cheese, onions and pepper sauce in slow cooker; mix thoroughly. Cover; cook on LOW 5 to 6 hours or on HIGH 2½ to 3 hours.

2. Uncover; sprinkle top with crackers and remaining ½ cup cheese. Cook, uncovered, on LOW 30 to 60 minutes or until cheese melts.   *Makes 4 to 6 servings*

Note: If desired, casserole may be spooned into a baking dish and garnished with additional cheese and crackers; bake 5 to 10 minutes in preheated 400°F oven.

Slow Roasted Potatoes

  16 small new potatoes
    3 tablespoons butter, cut into ⅛-inch pieces
    1 teaspoon paprika
  ½ teaspoon salt
  ¼ teaspoon garlic powder
    Black pepper to taste

1. Combine all ingredients in slow cooker; mix well. Cover; cook on LOW 7 hours or on HIGH 4 hours.

2. Remove potatoes with slotted spoon to serving dish; cover to keep warm. Add 1 to 2 tablespoons water to drippings and stir until well blended. Pour mixture over potatoes.

Makes 3 to 4 servings

Easy Dirty Rice

  ½ pound bulk Italian sausage or Italian-flavored turkey sausage
  2 cups water
  1 cup uncooked long grain rice
  1 large onion, finely chopped
  1 large green bell pepper, finely chopped
  ½ cup finely chopped celery
1½ teaspoons salt
  ½ teaspoon ground red pepper
  ½ cup chopped fresh parsley

1. Cook sausage in skillet, stirring to break up meat, until no longer pink. Place cooked sausage into slow cooker.

2. Stir in all remaining ingredients except parsley. Cover; cook on LOW 2 hours or until rice is tender. Stir in parsley. *Makes 4 servings*

Rustic Garlic Mashed Potatoes

  2 pounds baking potatoes, unpeeled and cut into ½-inch cubes
  ¼ cup water
  2 tablespoons butter, cut in ⅛-inch pieces
1¼ teaspoons salt
  ½ teaspoon garlic powder
  ¼ teaspoon black pepper
  1 cup milk

1. Place all ingredients except milk in slow cooker; toss to combine. Cover; cook on LOW 7 hours or on HIGH 4 hours.

2. Add milk to potatoes. Mash potatoes with potato masher or electric mixer until smooth. *Makes 5 servings*

Cran-Orange Acorn Squash

3 small carnival or acorn squash
5 tablespoons instant brown rice
3 tablespoons minced onion
3 tablespoons diced celery
3 tablespoons dried cranberries
 Pinch ground or dried sage
1 teaspoon butter, cut into bits
3 tablespoons orange juice
½ cup water

1. Slice off tops and bottoms of squash. Scoop out seeds and discard; set squash aside.

2. Combine rice, onion, celery, cranberries and sage in small bowl. Stuff squash with rice mixture; dot with butter. Pour 1 tablespoon orange juice into each squash over stuffing. Stand squash in slow cooker. Pour water into bottom of slow cooker.

3. Cover; cook on LOW 2½ hours or until squash is tender. *Makes 6 servings*

Helpful Hint: The skin of squash can defy even the sharpest knives. To make slicing easier, microwave the whole squash at HIGH 5 minutes to soften the skin.

Cran-Orange Acorn Squash

Swiss Cheese Scalloped Potatoes

   2 pounds baking potatoes, peeled and thinly sliced
   ½ cup finely chopped yellow onion
   ¼ teaspoon salt
   ¼ teaspoon ground nutmeg
   2 tablespoons butter, cut into ⅛-inch pieces
   ½ cup milk
   2 tablespoons all-purpose flour
   3 ounces Swiss cheese slices, torn into small pieces
   ¼ cup finely chopped green onions (optional)

1. Layer half the potatoes, ¼ cup onion, ⅛ teaspoon salt, ⅛ teaspoon nutmeg and 1 tablespoon butter in slow cooker. Repeat layers. Cover; cook on LOW 7 hours or on HIGH 4 hours. Remove potatoes with slotted spoon to serving dish.

2. Blend milk and flour in small bowl until smooth. Stir mixture into slow cooker. Add cheese; stir to combine. If slow cooker is on LOW, turn to HIGH. Cover; cook until slightly thickened, about 10 minutes. Stir. Pour cheese mixture over potatoes and serve. Garnish with chopped green onions, if desired.   *Makes 5 to 6 servings*

Swiss Cheese Scalloped Potatoes

Delicious Desserts & More

Peach Cobbler

   2 packages (16 ounces each) frozen peaches, thawed and drained
   ¾ cup sugar
   2 teaspoons ground cinnamon, divided
   ½ teaspoon ground nutmeg
   ¾ cup all-purpose flour
   1 tablespoon sugar
   6 tablespoons butter, cut into bits
     Whipped cream (if desired)

1. Combine peaches, sugar, 1½ teaspoons cinnamon and nutmeg in medium bowl. Place into slow cooker.

2. For topping, combine flour, sugar and remaining ½ teaspoon cinnamon in separate bowl. Cut in butter with pastry cutter or 2 knives until mixture resembles coarse crumbs. Sprinkle over peach mixture. Cover; cook on HIGH 2 hours. Serve with freshly whipped cream, if desired.

Makes 4 to 6 serving

Peach Cobbler

Steamed Pumpkin Cake

1½ cups all-purpose flour
1½ teaspoons baking powder
1½ teaspoons baking soda
 1 teaspoon ground cinnamon
½ teaspoon salt
¼ teaspoon ground cloves
½ cup unsalted butter, melted
 2 cups packed light brown sugar
 3 eggs, beaten
 1 can (15 ounces) pumpkin
   Sweetened whipped cream (optional)

1. Grease 2½ quart soufflé dish or baking pan that fits into slow cooker.

2. Combine flour, baking powder, baking soda, cinnamon, salt and cloves in medium bowl; set aside.

3. Beat butter, brown sugar and eggs in large bowl with electric mixer on medium speed until creamy. Beat in pumpkin. Stir in flour mixture. Spoon batter into prepared soufflé dish.

4. Fill slow cooker with 1 inch hot water. Make foil handles using technique described below. Place soufflé dish into slow cooker. Cover; cook on HIGH 3 to 3½ hours or until wooden toothpick inserted into center comes out clean.

5. Use foil handles to lift dish from slow cooker. Cool 15 minutes. Invert cake onto serving platter. Cut into wedges and serve with dollop of whipped cream, if desired.

Makes 12 servings

Foil Handles: Tear off three 18×2-inch strips of heavy foil or use regular foil folded to double thickness. Crisscross foil strip in spoke design as shown on page 7. Place soufflé dish in the center of strips. Pull foil strips up and over the dish.

Serving Suggestion: Enhance this old-fashioned dense cake with a topping of sautéed apples or pear slices, or a scoop of pumpkin ice cream.

Steamed Pumpkin Cake

Chocolate Chip Lemon Loaf

¾ cup granulated sugar
½ cup vegetable shortening
2 eggs, lightly beaten
1⅔ cups all-purpose flour
1½ teaspoons baking powder
¼ teaspoon salt
¾ cup milk
½ cup chocolate chips
   Peel of 1 lemon
   Juice of 1 lemon
¼ to ½ cup powdered sugar
   Melted chocolate (optional)

1. Grease 2-quart soufflé dish or 2-pound coffee can; set aside. Beat granulated sugar and shortening until blended. Add eggs, one at a time, mixing well after each addition.

2. Sift together flour, baking powder and salt. Add flour mixture and milk alternately to shortening mixture. Stir in chocolate chips and lemon peel.

3. Spoon batter into prepared dish. Cover with greased foil. Make foil handles as described on page 7 for easier removal of dish from slow cooker. Place dish into preheated slow cooker. Cook, covered with slow cooker lid slightly ajar to allow excess moisture to escape, on HIGH 1¾ to 2 hours or on LOW 3 to 4 hours or until edges are golden and knife inserted into center of loaf comes out clean. Use handles to lift dish from slow cooker; remove foil. Place loaf on wire rack to cool completely.

4. Combine lemon juice and ¼ cup powdered sugar in small bowl. Add more sugar as needed to reach desired consistency. Pour glaze over loaf. Drizzle loaf with melted chocolate, if desired.

Makes 8 servings

Chocolate Chip Lemon Loaf

Pecan-Cinnamon Pudding Cake

1⅓ cups all-purpose flour
½ cup granulated sugar
1½ teaspoons baking powder
1½ teaspoons ground cinnamon
⅔ cup milk
5 tablespoons butter or margarine, melted, divided
1 cup chopped pecans
1½ cups water
¾ cup packed brown sugar
Whipped cream (optional)

1. Stir together flour, granulated sugar, baking powder and cinnamon in medium bowl. Add milk and 3 tablespoons butter; mix just until blended. Stir in pecans. Spread on bottom of slow cooker.

2. Combine water, brown sugar and remaining 2 tablespoons butter in small saucepan; bring to a boil. Pour over batter in slow cooker.

3. Cover; cook on HIGH 2 to 2½ hours or until toothpick inserted into center of cake comes out clean. Let stand, uncovered, for 30 minutes.

4. Serve warm with whipped cream, if desired. *Makes 8 servings*

Peach-Pecan Upside Down Cake

   1 can (8½ ounces) peach slices
⅓ cup packed brown sugar
   2 tablespoons butter or margarine, melted
¼ cup chopped pecans
   1 package (16 ounces) pound cake mix
½ teaspoon almond extract
    Whipped cream (optional)

1. Generously grease a 7½-inch slow cooker bread-and-cake bake pan or casserole dish; set aside.

2. Drain peach slices, reserving 1 tablespoon of juice. Combine reserved peach juice, brown sugar and butter in prepared bake pan. Arrange peach slices on top of brown sugar mixture. Sprinkle with pecans.

3. Prepare cake mix according to package directions; stir in almond extract. Spread over peach mixture. Cover pan. Make foil handles as described on page 7 for easier removal of pan from slow cooker. Place pan into slow cooker. Cover; cook on HIGH 3 hours.

4. Use handles to lift pan from slow cooker. Cool, uncovered, on wire rack for 10 minutes. Run narrow spatula around sides of pan; invert onto serving plate. Serve warm with whipped cream, if desired.

Makes 10 servings

SLOW COOKING SECRET

Check the dish and pan required for making a dessert before getting started. Make sure it will fit into your-size slow cooker. Allow for a little space between the sides of the cooker and the pan or dish.

Chocolate Croissant Pudding

1½ cups milk
 3 eggs
½ cup sugar
¼ cup unsweetened cocoa powder
½ teaspoon vanilla
¼ teaspoon salt
 2 plain croissants, cut into 1-inch pieces
½ cup chocolate chips
¾ cup whipped cream (optional)

1. Beat milk, eggs, sugar, cocoa, vanilla and salt in medium bowl.

2. Grease 1-quart casserole. Layer half the croissants, chocolate chips and half the egg mixture in casserole. Repeat layers with remaining croissants and egg mixture.

3. Add rack to 5-quart slow cooker and pour in 1 cup water. Make foil handles as described on page 7 for easier removal of pan from slow cooker. Place casserole on rack. Cover; cook on LOW 3 to 4 hours.

4. Use handles to lift casserole from slow cooker. Top each serving with 2 tablespoons whipped cream, if desired.

Makes 6 servings

Chocolate Croissant Pudding

Apple-Date Crisp

6 cups thinly sliced peeled apples (about 6 medium apples, preferably
    Golden Delicious)
2 teaspoons lemon juice
⅓ cup chopped dates
1⅓ cups quick-cooking oats
½ cup all-purpose unbleached flour
½ cup packed light brown sugar
½ teaspoon ground cinnamon
¼ teaspoon ground ginger
¼ teaspoon salt
    Pinch ground nutmeg
    Pinch ground cloves (optional)
¼ cup (½ stick) cold butter, cut into small pieces

1. Spray slow cooker with nonstick cooking spray. Place apples in a medium bowl. Sprinkle with lemon juice; toss to coat. Add dates and mix well. Transfer apple mixture to slow cooker.

2. Combine oats, flour, brown sugar, cinnamon, ginger, salt, nutmeg and cloves, if desired, in medium bowl. Cut in butter with pastry blender or two knives until mixture resembles coarse crumbs.

3. Pour oat mixture into slow cooker over apples; smooth top. Cover; cook on HIGH about 2 hours or on LOW about 4 hours. *Makes 6 servings*

Apple-Date Crisp

Luscious Pecan Bread Pudding

        3 cups French bread cubes
        3 tablespoons chopped pecans, toasted
    2¼ cups low-fat (1%) milk
        2 eggs, beaten
        ½ cup sugar
        1 teaspoon vanilla
        ¾ teaspoon ground cinnamon, divided
        ¾ cup reduced-calorie cranberry juice cocktail
    1½ cups frozen pitted tart cherries
        2 tablespoons sugar substitute

1. Toss bread cubes and pecans in soufflé dish. Combine milk, eggs, sugar, vanilla and ½ teaspoon cinnamon in large bowl. Pour over bread mixture in soufflé dish. Cover tightly with foil.

2. Make foil handles (see page 7). Place soufflé dish into slow cooker. Pour hot water into slow cooker to come about 1½ inches from top of soufflé dish. Cover; cook on LOW 2 to 3 hours.

3. Meanwhile, stir together cranberry juice and remaining ¼ teaspoon cinnamon in small saucepan; stir in frozen cherries. Bring sauce to a boil over medium heat, about 5 minutes. Remove from heat. Stir in sugar substitute.

4. Lift dish from slow cooker with foil handles. Serve bread pudding with cherry sauce.

Makes 6 servings

Mixed Berry Cobbler

    1 package (16 ounces) frozen mixed berries
    ¾ cup granulated sugar
    2 tablespoons quick-cooking tapioca
    2 teaspoons grated fresh lemon peel
  1½ cups all-purpose flour
    ½ cup packed brown sugar
  2¼ teaspoons baking powder
    ¼ teaspoon ground nutmeg
    ¾ cup milk
    ⅓ cup butter or margarine, melted
    Ice cream (optional)

1. Stir together berries, granulated sugar, tapioca and lemon peel in a slow cooker.

2. Combine flour, brown sugar, baking powder and nutmeg in medium bowl. Add milk and butter; stir just until blended. Drop spoonfuls on top of berry mixture.

3. Cover; cook on LOW 4 hours. Uncover; let stand about 30 minutes.

4. Serve with ice cream, if desired.

Makes 8 servings

SLOW COOKING SECRET

When making desserts in the slow cooker be sure to cook at the heat setting listed in the recipe. Unlike other slow cooker dishes such as soups and stews that can be cooked at variable heat settings, desserts may not cook correctly on a setting other that the one listed.

Pumpkin-Cranberry Custard

1 can (30 ounces) pumpkin pie filling
1 can (12 ounces) evaporated milk
1 cup dried cranberries
4 eggs, beaten
1 cup crushed or whole ginger snap cookies (optional)
Whipped cream (optional)

1. Combine pumpkin, evaporated milk, cranberries and eggs in slow cooker; mix thoroughly. Cover; cook on HIGH 4 to 4½ hours.

2. Serve with crushed or whole ginger snaps and whipped cream, if desired.

Make 4 to 6 servings

Cherry Rice Pudding

1½ cups milk
1 cup hot cooked rice
3 eggs, beaten
½ cup sugar
¼ cup dried cherries or cranberries
½ teaspoon almond extract
¼ teaspoon salt

1. Combine all ingredients in large bowl. Pour mixture into greased 1½-quart casserole. Cover with foil. Add rack to 5-quart slow cooker and pour in 1 cup water. Make foil handles as described on page 7. Place casserole on rack. Cover; cook on LOW 4 to 5 hours.

2. Use foil handles to lift casserole from slow cooker. Let stand 15 minutes before serving.

Makes 6 servings

Pumpkin-Cranberry Custard

Coconut Rice Pudding

2 cups water
1 cup uncooked long grain rice
1 tablespoon unsalted butter
Pinch salt
18 ounces evaporated milk
1 can (14 ounces) cream of coconut
½ cup golden raisins
3 egg yolks, beaten
Peel of 2 limes
1 teaspoon vanilla extract
Toasted shredded coconut (optional)

1. Place water, rice, butter and salt in medium saucepan. Bring to a rolling boil over high heat, stirring frequently. Reduce heat to low. Cover; cook 10 to 12 minutes. Remove from heat. Cover and let stand 5 minutes.

2. Meanwhile, spray slow cooker with nonstick cooking spray. Add evaporated milk, cream of coconut, raisins, egg yolks, lime peel and vanilla extract; mix well. Add rice; stir to combine. Cover; cook on LOW 4 hours or on HIGH 2 hours. Stir every 30 minutes, if possible.

3. Pudding will thicken as it cools. Garnish with toasted shredded coconut, if desired.

Makes 6 (¾-cup) servings

Coconut Rice Pudding

Cherry Flan

 5 eggs
½ cup sugar
½ teaspoon salt
¾ cup flour
 1 can (12 ounces) evaporated milk
 1 teaspoon vanilla
 1 bag (16 ounces) frozen, pitted dark sweet cherries, thawed
    Sweetened whipped cream or cherry vanilla ice cream (optional)

1. Grease inside of slow cooker.

2. Beat eggs, sugar and salt in large bowl of electric mixer at high speed until thick. Add flour; stir until smooth. Stir in evaporated milk and vanilla.

3. Pour batter into prepared slow cooker. Place cherries evenly over batter. Cover; cook on LOW 3½ to 4 hours or until flan is set.

4. Serve warm with whipped cream or ice cream, if desired.   *Makes 6 servings*

Note: This yummy dessert is like a custard and a cake mixed together. It is best served warm and is especially delicious when topped with whipped cream or ice cream.

Pineapple Rice Pudding

1 can (20 ounces) crushed pineapple in juice, undrained
1 can (13½ ounces) coconut milk
1 can (12 ounces) nonfat evaporated milk
¾ cup uncooked arborio rice
2 eggs, lightly beaten
¼ cup sugar
¼ cup packed light brown sugar
½ teaspoon cinnamon
¼ teaspoon ground nutmeg
¼ teaspoon salt
  Whipped topping
  Toasted coconut for garnish* (optional)

To toast coconut, spread evenly on cookie sheet. Toast in preheated 350°F oven 7 minutes. Stir and toast 1 to 2 minutes more or until light golden brown.

1. Place pineapple with juice, coconut milk, evaporated milk, rice, eggs, sugar, brown sugar, cinnamon, nutmeg and salt into slow cooker; mix well. Cover; cook on HIGH 3 to 4 hours or until thickened and rice is cooked.

2. Remove cover and stir to mix thoroughly. Serve warm or chilled with whipped topping. Garnish with coconut, if desired. *Makes about 8 (1 cup) servings*

SLOW COOKING SECRET

To avoid curdling of milk in slow cooker recipes, use evaporated milk or heavy cream.

Baked Ginger Apples

   4 large Red Delicious apples
   ½ cup (1 stick) unsalted butter, melted
   ⅓ cup chopped macadamia nuts
   ¼ cup chopped dried apricots
   2 tablespoons finely chopped crystallized ginger
   1 tablespoon dark brown sugar
   ¾ cup brandy
   ½ cup vanilla pudding and pie filling mix
   2 cups heavy cream

1. Slice tops off apples and core. Combine butter, macadamia nuts, apricots, ginger and brown sugar in medium bowl. Fill apples with nut mixture. Place apples in slow cooker. Pour brandy into slow cooker. Cover; cook on LOW 4 hours or on HIGH 2 hours.

2. Gently remove apples from slow cooker; set aside and keep warm. Combine pudding mix and cream in small bowl. Add to slow cooker; stir to combine with brandy mixture. Cover; cook on HIGH 30 minutes. Stir until smooth. Return apples in slow cooker and keep warm until ready to serve.

3. Serve apples with cream mixture.   *Makes 4 servings*

Baked Ginger Apple

Cran-Apple Orange Conserve

>   2 medium oranges
>   5 large tart apples, peeled, cored and chopped
>   2 cups sugar
>   1½ cups fresh cranberries
>   1 tablespoon grated fresh lemon peel
>   Pound cake

1. Remove a thin slice from both ends of both oranges for easier chopping. Finely chop unpeeled oranges and remove any seeds (about 2 cups).

2. Combine oranges, apples, sugar, cranberries and lemon peel in slow cooker. Cover; cook on HIGH 4 hours. Slightly crush fruit with potato masher.

3. Cook, uncovered, on HIGH 2 to 2½ hours or until very thick, stirring occasionally to prevent sticking. Cool at least 2 hours.

4. Serve with pound cake.   *Makes about 5 cups*

Serving Suggestion: Fruit conserve can also be served with roast pork or poultry.

Chunky Vanilla Pears

>   1¼ pounds ripe pears, peeled and diced
>   8 dried orange essence plums, cut into quarters
>   ¼ cup granulated sugar
>   1 tablespoon lemon juice
>   ½ teaspoon vanilla

1. Combine all ingredients except vanilla in slow cooker. Cover; cook 1 hour on HIGH.

2. Stir in vanilla. Serve hot or at room temperature with roasted ham, pork, chicken or lamb. Or, serve as a dessert sauce over ice cream, angel food cake or pound cake.   *Makes 2 cups*

Cran-Apple Orange Conserve

Spiced Plums and Pears

2 cans (29 ounces each) sliced pears in heavy syrup, undrained
2 pounds black or red plums (about 12 to 14), pitted and sliced
1 cup packed brown sugar
1 teaspoon ground cinnamon
½ teaspoon ground ginger
¼ teaspoon grated lemon peel
2 tablespoons cornstarch
2 tablespoons water
   Pound cake or ice cream
   Whipped topping

1. Cut pear slices in half with spoon. Place pears, plums, sugar, cinnamon, ginger and lemon peel in slow cooker. Cover; cook on HIGH 4 hours.

2. Combine cornstarch and water to make smooth paste. Stir into slow cooker. Cook on HIGH until slightly thickened.

3. Serve warm or at room temperature over pound cake with whipped topping.

Makes 6 to 8 servings

Serving Suggestion: Also, serve as a condiment with baked ham, roast pork or roast turkey.

Sweet & Hot Onion Relish

3 cups chopped onion
½ cup mild salsa
½ cup packed dark brown sugar
1 tablespoon cider vinegar
¼ to ½ teaspoon red pepper flakes

1. Combine all ingredients in slow cooker. Cover; cook on LOW 7 to 8 hours or on HIGH 3 to 4 hours until onions are very tender.

2. Serve at room temperature as a condiment for roast pork or chicken or chilled over cream cheese.

Makes 1½ cups relish

Gingered Pineapple and Cranberries

    2 cans (20 ounces) pineapple tidbits in juice, undrained
    1 cup dried sweetened cherry-flavored cranberries
    ½ cup brown sugar
    1 teaspoon curry powder, divided
    1 teaspoon grated fresh ginger, divided
    ¼ teaspoon red pepper flakes
    2 tablespoons water
    1 tablespoon cornstarch

1. Place pineapple with juice, cranberries, brown sugar, ½ teaspoon curry, ½ teaspoon ginger and pepper flakes into slow cooker. Cover; cook on HIGH 3 hours.

2. Combine water, cornstarch, remaining ½ teaspoon curry and ½ teaspoon ginger in small bowl; stir until cornstarch is dissolved. Add to pineapple mixture; cook on HIGH 15 minutes or until thickened. *Makes 4 ½ cups*

Variation: Substitute 2 cans (20 ounces each) pineapple tidbits in heavy syrup for pineapple and brown sugar.

Spicy Apple Butter

    5 pounds tart cooking apples (such as Macintosh, Granny Smith, Rome Beauty or York Imperial), peeled, cored and quartered (about 10 large apples)
    1 cup sugar
    ½ cup apple juice
    2 teaspoons ground cinnamon
    ½ teaspoon ground cloves
    ½ teaspoon ground allspice

1. Combine all ingredients in slow cooker. Cover; cook on LOW 8 to 10 hours or until apples are very tender.

2. Mash apples with potato masher. Cook, uncovered, on LOW 2 hours or until mixture is very thick, stirring occasionally to prevent sticking. *Makes about 6 cups*

Red Pepper Relish

    2 large red bell peppers, cut into thin strips
    1 small Vidalia or other sweet onion, thinly sliced
    3 tablespoons cider vinegar
    2 tablespoons packed light brown sugar
    1 tablespoon vegetable oil
    1 tablespoon honey
    ¼ teaspoon salt
    ¼ teaspoon dried thyme leaves
    ¼ teaspoon red pepper flakes
    ¼ teaspoon black pepper

Combine all ingredients in slow cooker; mix well. Cover; cook on LOW 4 hours.

Makes 4 servings

Chunky Sweet Spiced Apple Butter

    4 cups (about 1¼ pounds) chopped Granny Smith apples
    ¾ cup packed dark brown sugar
    2 tablespoons balsamic vinegar
    ¼ cup butter, divided
    1 tablespoon ground cinnamon
    ¼ teaspoon ground cloves
    ½ teaspoon salt
  1½ teaspoons vanilla

1. Combine apples, sugar, vinegar, 2 tablespoons butter, cinnamon, cloves and salt in slow cooker. Cover; cook on LOW 8 hours.

2. Stir in remaining 2 tablespoons butter and vanilla. Cool completely.

Makes 2 cups

Serving Suggestion: Serve with roasted meats or toasted English muffins.

Red Pepper Relish

INDEX

METRIC CONVERSION CHART

VOLUME MEASUREMENTS (dry)

1/8 teaspoon = 0.5 mL
1/4 teaspoon = 1 mL
1/2 teaspoon = 2 mL
3/4 teaspoon = 4 mL
1 teaspoon = 5 mL
1 tablespoon = 15 mL
2 tablespoons = 30 mL
1/4 cup = 60 mL
1/3 cup = 75 mL
1/2 cup = 125 mL
2/3 cup = 150 mL
3/4 cup = 175 mL
1 cup = 250 mL
2 cups = 1 pint = 500 mL
3 cups = 750 mL
4 cups = 1 quart = 1 L

VOLUME MEASUREMENTS (fluid)

1 fluid ounce (2 tablespoons) = 30 mL
4 fluid ounces (1/2 cup) = 125 mL
8 fluid ounces (1 cup) = 250 mL
12 fluid ounces (1 1/2 cups) = 375 mL
16 fluid ounces (2 cups) = 500 mL

WEIGHTS (mass)

1/2 ounce = 15 g
1 ounce = 30 g
3 ounces = 90 g
4 ounces = 120 g
8 ounces = 225 g
10 ounces = 285 g
12 ounces = 360 g
16 ounces = 1 pound = 450 g

DIMENSIONS

1/16 inch = 2 mm
1/8 inch = 3 mm
1/4 inch = 6 mm
1/2 inch = 1.5 cm
3/4 inch = 2 cm
1 inch = 2.5 cm

OVEN TEMPERATURES

250°F = 120°C
275°F = 140°C
300°F = 150°C
325°F = 160°C
350°F = 180°C
375°F = 190°C
400°F = 200°C
425°F = 220°C
450°F = 230°C

BAKING PAN SIZES

Utensil	Size in Inches/Quarts	Metric Volume	Size in Centimeters
Baking or Cake Pan (square or rectangular)	8×8×2	2 L	20×20×5
	9×9×2	2.5 L	23×23×5
	12×8×2	3 L	30×20×5
	13×9×2	3.5 L	33×23×5
Loaf Pan	8×4×3	1.5 L	20×10×7
	9×5×3	2 L	23×13×7
Round Layer Cake Pan	8×1½	1.2 L	20×4
	9×1½	1.5 L	23×4
Pie Plate	8×1¼	750 mL	20×3
	9×1¼	1 L	23×3
Baking Dish or Casserole	1 quart	1 L	—
	1½ quart	1.5 L	—
	2 quart	2 L	—